LITERARY THEORY
AND ENGLISH
TEACHING

Open University Press

English, Language, and Education series

General Editor: Anthony Adams

Lecturer in Education, University of Cambridge

This series is concerned with all aspects of language in education from the primary school to the tertiary sector. Its authors are experienced educators who examine both principles and practice of English subject teaching and language across the curriculum in the context of current educational and societal developments.

TITLES IN THE SERIES

Time for Drama: A Handbook for Secondary Teachers
Roma Burgess and Pamela Gaudry

Computers and Literacy
Daniel Chandler and Stephen Marcus (eds)

Readers, Texts, Teachers
Emrys Evans and Bill Corcoran (eds.)

Children Talk About Books: Seeing Themselves as Readers
Donald Fry

Literary Theory and English Teaching
Peter Griffith

Assessing English
Brian Johnston

The English Department in a Changing World
Richard Knott

Teaching Literature for Examinations
Robert Protherough

Developing Response to Fiction
Robert Protherough

Microcomputers and the Language Arts
Brent Robinson

English Teaching in Perspective (2nd Edn.)
Ken Watson

The Quality of Writing
Andrew Wilkinson

The Writing of Writing
Andrew Wilkinson (ed.)

In preparation

English Teaching: Programmes and Policies
Anthony Adams and Esmor Jones

LITERARY THEORY AND ENGLISH TEACHING

Peter Griffith

Open University Press

Milton Keynes · Philadelphia

Open University Press
Open University Educational Enterprises Limited
12 Cofferidge Close
Stony Stratford
Milton Keynes MK11 1BY, England
and

242 Cherry Street
Philadelphia, PA 19106, USA

First Published 1987

PR
33
G84
1987

British Library Cataloguing in Publication Data
Griffith, Peter, *1951–*
    Literary theory and English teaching—
      (English, language, and education series)
    1. English literature—History and criticism   2. Criticism
    I. Title   II. Series
    820.9   PR57

    ISBN 0–335–15250–3

Library of Congress Cataloging-in-Publication Data

Griffith, Peter.
    Literaray theory and English teaching.

    (English, language, and education series)
    Bibliography: p.
    includes index.
    1. English literature—Study and teaching.
    2. Literature—History and criticism—Theory, etc.
    I. Title.
    PR33.G84   1987   807'.12   86–43212

    ISBN 0–335–15250–3 (pbk.)

Text design by Clarke Williams
Typeset by Thomson Litho Ltd., East Kilbride, Scotland
Printed in Great Britain by Thomson Litho Ltd., East Kilbride, Scotland

For Diana, Emily, Laura and Lorna
for all the books we have read together.

Contents

Preface

Since this book is intended as introductory to a number of theories of literature, it may seem excessive to provide it also with an introductory preface. However, there are two comments which may help the intending reader at this point.

The first concerns the use and definition of technical terms. I have tried to keep the use of such terms to a minimum, and to define each one on its first appearance. However, Chapter 2 bristles with them, and it may be some comfort to the reader to know that the incidence drops thereafter. To avoid the necessity for constantly hunting back, I have provided a very brief glossary, which is intended to provide first aid rather than to be definitive.

The second comment that must be made concerns the form of third-person pronouns and adjectives used in this book. 'He or she' is cumbersome, and 's/he' untidy. My virtuous, if naïve, intention was therefore to alternate genders as between chapters. But, since linguistic form is an outcome of social practice, it soon became apparent that this was having curious effects upon the meaning of what was being written. Try changing 'he' to 'she' throughout the discussion of Lacan, and you will see what I mean. I have therefore kept more or less to my original plan in respect of my own comments, but retained the exclusive use of the masculine form when the theory under discussion seemed to demand it. The resulting distribution, though undoubtedly untidy, may also have something to tell the attentive reader about the nature of various literary theories.

Acknowledgements

I should like to thank Anthony Adams, John Coombes, Dominic Newbould and Diana Griffith for their various and helpful comments on the text of this book. Convention requires me to state that I am solely responsible for any errors, distortions or omissions, and this I hereby do. Much literary theory, however, would dispute this assertion.

General Editor's Introduction

In 1985, the National Association for the Teaching of English invited Terry Eagleton, the well-known teacher of English literature and literary theory from Oxford University, to address its annual conference at Nottingham. This is one of the few occasions in recent years when a distinguished figure in the world of university English teaching has engaged in a dialogue with a representative group of classroom teachers of English. Indeed, as much in the field of literary study has become more specialized and more theoretical, the gap between what is taught in classrooms (including in sixth form and further education) and what is taught in many English faculties in higher education has become ever wider. The language itself is specialized and may well seem arcane to those who, like myself, were brought up in an earlier generation of literary studies where 'lit.crit.' supported by Practical Criticism ruled.

This was not always the case. In previous generations when the leading figures in university teaching were such people as Sir Walter Raleigh, or Quiller-Couch, the contact was much greater, at least with the then grammar schools. The English Association was thriving and numbered many classroom teachers amongst its members who attended its annual lectures—still, incidentally, a valuable occasion. Even when British criticism was dominated by the work of F. R. Leavis, the mediation of his influence through the work of Denys Thompson (especially through his editorship of 'The Use of English') ensured that many teachers of English were in direct touch with the work going on in the universities.

Such teachers were still, of course, working in grammar school English departments. The coming of comprehensive education coincided with upheavals in the field of English teaching in the universities, which many teachers of English have since been trying to take on board. The 'new' science of linguistics was a case in point in the 1960s when stylistics began to take over from the tradition of literary criticism. Some books sought to bridge the gap, notably Henry Widdowson's *Stylistics and the Teaching of Literature* and I remember helping to staff a DES course in the early 1970s which focused upon the role of stylistics in classroom teaching at which Widdowson was a prominent, and controversial, staff member.

Peter Griffith's book sets out to bring all this up to date for the late 1980s. His brief was that we wanted something that would enable the concerned, but new, reader in this field, especially the classroom teacher of English, to understand and apply modern critical theory to his or her own teaching, especially at senior secondary level. We wanted all this to embrace structuralist and post-structuralist approaches, to look at narratology, to examine Marxist critical theory, amongst other things. To my knowledge, there is no book that really does this at the appropriate level at the present time. The nearest is Eagleton's own *Literary Theory* but that is written from a very particular standpoint and this was something we wanted Griffith to avoid. And all this, a study (not just a survey) of the contending current literary theories in higher education, was to be presented within the confines of a relatively short book.

As General Editor, I am very happy with what he has produced. It seems to me to be admirably balanced in its outlook and to carry out exactly the task that I set its author. He shows himself to be a skilled mediator of unfamiliar, and at times difficult, ideas to readers (such as myself) who come to many of them in a naïve frame of mind.

But Griffith does more than this. He shows that the roots of much of current literary theory can be traced in the past history of our culture, especially back to the work of linguistics with particular reference to the seminal (in every sense of the word) work of Saussure, and I think that he shows convincingly the relevance of these kinds of approaches to litera- ture for the teaching of English in the comprehensive school. Much modern theory can lead to an approach to literature which is essentially against the élitism which traditional twentieth-century criticism often appeared to be. (I say 'appeared' because it was by no means always so and, amongst other things, Griffith's brief discussion of the work of Leavis shows that to have been by no means always so élitist as it has been thought to be.)

But we have here, I believe, an emergent rationale for the teaching of English in the comprehensive curriculum and a powerful statement for the retention of 'literature' (understood in a wider than the traditional sense) as an important element within that curriculum. There is much ammunition for us, as teachers of literature, in these pages in the increasing pressures towards a more skills-based and limitedly utilitarian model of teaching.

A surprise to me when I read the typescript was Chapter 7, which shows that the kinds of approaches presented here have relevance not only to the later stages of education but are also applicable with younger students, in the early secondary years, or even in the primary school. By taking as his fundamental text for exegesis Twain's *The Adventures of Tom Sawyer*, a decision he effectively explains and defends in the final chapter, rather than something more within the official canon of 'good literature', like Twain's *Huckleberry Finn*, Griffith shows how modern criticism can be illuminating at a range of stages in education from primary school to university. It is a bold and convincing demonstration.

It should be said, however, that the book, while admirably clear, is not always easy to read. The ideas it presents are often complex and frequently controversial. The reader will discover that it makes demands not only of concentration but also of adjustment. For some of us, many of the assumptions of our earlier literary education will come under severe and

cogent scrutiny—another word that I use in this context quite deliber-
ately. Every age may need to remake its literary criticism in terms of its
own needs and ideologies. This was what Leavis achieved in *Scrutiny*; it is
what is being achieved in the works of the theorists that Griffith discusses
here.

Much of the important work of English teaching and the theory
underlying it has passed in recent years from university English departments to Education departments. This series has published already some
of the recent work of the most distinguished practitioners in these fields.
But there is a gap becoming fixed between faculties of English and
faculties of Education. It is important that we begin to talk to each other
again. That is why the series is called 'English, Language, and Education'
with the intention to lay stress upon each of the elements within it. The
current volume is a more theoretical one than some of the others that we
have published already: its stress appears to be very much on the area of
'English' but it is just as relevant to 'Language' and to 'Education'. I hope
that we shall have the opportunity to publish works of similar distinction
in this field in the future.

Anthony Adams

1 Language and literature: an introduction

This book is written at a time when major changes are occurring in education: changes in respect of financing, of control and, not entirely unconnected with these, changes in the design and management of the curriculum. Where 'English' as a curricular entity is concerned, there are further and specific pressures at work. Concern about 'standards', mainly of orthography and grammar, was part of the original impetus towards the commissioning of the Bullock Report, and was subsequently heightened (if not exactly focused) by the so-called 'Great Debate' in education and subsequent political pronouncements. This process can be seen as a continuous assault upon the always tenuous progressive consensus within the subject that emerged during the 1960s.

But this consensus was being modified by other pressures as well. At the beginning of the century English Literature was seen as a canon of great works, with a vital (if somewhat belated) role to play in the formation of a national consciousness. With hindsight, it is possible to say that the tenets of F. R. Leavis, greatly influential in the postwar teaching of English, modified rather than challenged this position. Within English teaching, however, concern shifted from the study of great works to an emphasis on the primary value of the individual development, both cognitive and affective, of each pupil. The study of literature was seen as instrumental in such a process, a means rather than an end.

The resulting paradox has been described by Rosen (in conversation) as Leavisite Leninism, and by Eagleton (in print) as left-Leavisite. Both are attempting to capture the situation of the teacher who, on the one hand, clings to a largely conservative belief in the beneficial effects of reading good books and, on the other, sustains a broadly progressive faith in the interconnectedness of individual personal development and beneficial social change. In one respect, however, both Rosen's and

Eagleton's labels fail to meet the case. Neither Bolshevism nor German philosophy could be said to lack a theoretical base. But to speak of 'literary theory' within the world of English teaching was, it seemed, to use an oxymoron.

During this period, though, literary theory was being produced, re-defined, argued over, in France, in Germany, in Austria and, in a some-what different guise, in America. The people who were doing this were to be found in universities, but had degrees in linguistics or philosophy or sociology at least as often as they had in literature. Over the past twenty-five years, many of their works have been translated into English, though often out of sequence one with another. The response of literature departments in British universities to these developments has ranged from constructive engagement to moral panic. Both responses, however, recognize the powerful implications that much recent theory has for the practice of English teaching, not least in schools. There can be no better time than the present, therefore, to attempt an assessment of the utility of literary theory to the practice of education.

Let me provide an example of what I propose by looking at a classic paper by Jakobson (1960) on the component elements of a speech event. He represents these in the following way:

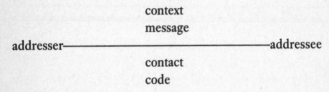

Figure 1   Elements of a speech event (Jakobson 1960)

Some of these terms are self-explanatory, so that the *addresser* is the person speaking and the *addressee* the person spoken to. It can seem a simple exercise, then, to substitute 'author' and 'reader' for these terms, and to say that the message is the text of the book that passes between them or, more precisely, all the meanings it contains. But Jakobson's model is more complex than this. For a *message* to be successfully trans-mitted there has also to be *contact*, which is a channel of communication (in the case we are looking at, the printed book); *code*, a series of recogniz-able symbols (in this case, Standard English as represented by con-ventional English orthography); and *context*, a mutually shared perception of situation (and I find it increasingly hard to specify what this may be).

The point that Jakobson is making is that the message is not simple, transparent, self-explanatory; it is something that is realized only in conjunction with contact, code, and context. Change any one of these, and you change the message as well.

Let us consider how many of these elements can reasonably be seen as unproblematic when the activity (or speech event) consists of the study of a work of literature in a British classroom towards the end of the twentieth century. The addresser will not be someone that is personally known— she or he may be from another country, or dead, or both. The addressees will almost certainly not be the intended recipients of the message, since, although writing a set text for schools is one of the few ways in which to become even moderately rich by being published, it is a coup that is particularly difficult to bring off, and is most often achieved by accident. A more typical situation (let us take a book like Mark Twain's *The Adventures of Tom Sawyer*) is a text where the addresser is a nineteenth-century American, and the addressees (as envisaged by him) a popular Anglo-American audience of the 1870s. Contact may be supposed to be less of a problem; suppose, though, that is is the first book without illustrations that the pupil has had to cope with, or that it is printed in small type in the interests of economy, or even that the book is falling to bits because the school cannot afford to replace it, or that it is shared with one or more other pupils. The code may be familiar in the sense that the book is written in English, but it will contain unfamiliar lexical items (such as 'bluff' for small cliff) a certain amount of deviant orthography to represent the speech of Huckleberry Finn, and a syntax more complex than some of its readers have been required to process before. And what can be said about the context? It is Tuesday afternoon, the mower is making one of its occasional visits to the grass outside, the class next door is getting noisy, the book is being studied for a new examination, and the likelihood that an exam pass will lead to future employment in the vicinity is remote. What set of meanings will emerge here?

So far I have only presented half of Jakobson's communication model. Corresponding to each element in the model there is a function, and the functions can be represented as follows:

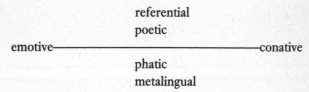

Figure 2   Functions in a speech event (Jakobson 1960)

What Jakobson means by this second set of terms is that, if in a given speech event the focus is on the addresser ('How sad I am!') then the function is primarily *emotive*. If the focus is on the addressee ('Read the following three chapters') its function, a *conative* one, is to control or influence her or him in some way. When contact predominates ('Can you hear me, mother?') the function is *phatic*, checking that communication is being established. With code, a *metalingual* function carries out a some-what similar activity but in respect of the code ('Excuse me, can you speak English?'). In the case of context, the *referential* function is concerned with the environment in which the speech event is taking place ('The two elements are forming a compound in the test-tube'). And, in Jakobson's view, when the focus is on the message itself as a self-conscious artefact, this is when we truly get the *poetic* function of language.

It is important to stress two things at this point. Jakobson was thinking primarily of lyric poetry in the above model rather than, say, a realistic novel or a naturalistic drama, though his model applies in principle to all these, and in lyric poetry the devices of rhyme, rhythm and, often, diction as well, call attention to the stylized nature of the utterance. But Jakobson was also writing as an inheritor of Russian formalism, in which the literariness of literature consisted precisely of the way in which it de-familiarized the language, making its audience aware of the constructed nature of what it was reading, so that the medium was no longer trans-parent. In this sense the message of literature is neither more nor less than 'What you are reading is literature'.

But, just as different functional utterances are related primarily to one part or another of Jakobson's communicative model of speech events, so different approaches to the study of literature have stressed different parts of the model as well. For instance, the kind of biographical approach that claims that literature is the product of an individual genius, whose life and inner experiences can be recaptured by a diligent study of his literary output, is directing its pedagogical thrust at the addresser. The kind of literature teaching that says that its justification lies in the beneficial moral effects of reading good books is focusing on the addressee. A bibliophile, concerned with first editions and fine bindings, is someone concentrating on the contact. The kind of literary approach that is concerned with assigning works to a period, with identifying the thumbprints of 'back-ground' on 'style', is directing particular attention to the code. The kind of comment that says that literature teaching is a way of defusing protest, an ideological confidence trick in which dominant social values are incul-cated, is offering an analysis directed at the context. And a traditional aesthete, insisting that the only proper activity in relation to literature is to appreciate its beauty, is claiming that the only valid area of literary study is that which relates to the message.

In this last paragraph I have simplified, perhaps even parodied, in order to illustrate a model of a process. Positions that are adopted by real people in real life are often more complex and multiple—and this is far from being a criticism, it seems to me. To illustrate what I have in mind in speaking of complexity, I propose looking at a literary critical essay by F. R. Leavis, a critic whose practices, concerns, and idiosyncracies have been highly influential in secondary and tertiary English teaching in this country in the post-war years. It would be misleading of me to claim that the following passages have been selected merely at random, but they could certainly be paralled by any number of similar ones. They come from an essay on T. S. Eliot's 'Four Quartets', an essay which was published in 1969. The first passage that I have selected, however, begins with a reference to Coriolanus in Eliot's poem 'A Cooking Egg'.

> The irony here conveys criticism of some kind (I imagine) of the Honour, the Pride, that the name of Coriolanus evokes, but the later passages ... suggest a new sense in the poet that there was too much Coriolanus in the irony. There is no touch of superiority in 'The Hollow Men'; the poet himself is too much the broken Coriolanus to be ironical in any way ... Nor does he revert to the old kind of irony in the unfinished sequence he called, significantly, *Coriolan*, though the account I have given of those poems is that they are the nearest thing we can expect in our age to distinguished satiric poetry. The figure of Coriolanus was lodged deep in Eliot's imag-
> ination ...   (p. 114)

In this relatively brief passage there are references to the poet, the addresser, which suggest that Leavis can confidently state what was lodged in this person's imagination, and can detect the point in his life at which Eliot decided to renounce an earlier use of irony. But the addressee is also called into play ('*We* can expect') and the context is evoked, both explicitly, in the phrase 'in our age', and, more implicitly, in the suggestion that the name of Coriolanus evokes honour and pride. The categorization of *Coriolan* as distinguished satiric poetry is a statement about code, and, to find a statement about message, I have to move on to the end of Leavis's paragraph:

> The point I want to make regards the nature of Eliot's genius. He has ... the power of giving concrete definition to ... feelings and apprehensions ... that have seemed to him peculiarly significant elements in his most private experience. But what goes with this power in the fully mature Eliot is the power of searching and sustained thought; thought that is not a matter of reflecting poetically (to use Eliot's own dismissing phrase), but thought that requires for its definition and conduct means and procedures
> that are essentially poetic.   (p. 115)

Starting with a claim to access to Eliot's most private experience (a definitive addresser-related comment) in the first sentence, Leavis moves on in the second sentence to extol 'means and procedures that are essentially poetic'—the very essence of what the category 'poetic' in Jakobson's scheme was all about. And, presumably, the chief reason I can adduce for the absence of reference to contact as a category in all this is that Leavis, whatever his other limitations, was no vulgar materialist.

To some people, the fact that Leavis shifted his ground so readily between these five categories is proof enough that he is a non-theoretical critic—in fact an anti-theoretical one—and therefore a thoroughly bad thing. I find such a criticism somewhat sweeping—there seems to me no harm, but rather good, in attempting to deal with the whole communicative process—but I certainly think that the constant confusion of categories, without pausing to distinguish them in any way, gravely vitiates the whole enterprise.

The rest of this book is, amongst other things, an attempt to provide some theoretical underpinning for the study of literature as a communicative process carried out within the confines of a formal educational system. It cannot attempt to provide a full and comprehensive account of literary theory up to the present day. Even with those theories and theorists that are discussed, my approach has been both radically selective and pragmatic: I have attempted to fillet out from the works in question those aspects that can most usefully and effectively be applied to a consideration of the teaching process.

The succeeding chapters of this book, and in particular the earlier ones, reflect in some of their themes the terms employed by Jakobson in the diagrams reproduced above. This has the advantage of emphasizing the focus of discussion in each case, but it also introduces an inevitable element of distortion and simplification, since literary theorists, whatever their professed intention, do not always treat each element of the communicative process in careful isolation any more than literary critics do. It will also be seen later that the model of the process that Jakobson employed has itself been called into question by subsequent theorists, so that it should be treated, in the context of this book at least, as a crutch which the reader eventually learns to throw away.

To a very limited extent the organization of this book is a chronological one, in that the work of the structuralists discussed in Chapter 2 preceded that of the post-structuralists who are examined in succeeding chapters. Too much reliance should not be placed upon this schematization, however. Some structuralists radically changed the bases of their arguments, whereas others undertook a progressive refinement of their previous positions. Other schools of thought, such as those dealing with the role of the reader and discussed in Chapter 3, carried out their work in relative isolation from the other intellectual traditions looked at here. To the degree that this book imposes a pattern of organization upon its basic material, then, it can be seen as working away from the horizontal axis of addresser——message——addressee that Jakobson proposed, and progressing vertically instead through the other categories in his model towards others that lie outside it.

In one important respect, the text of this book is determined by the material it deals with. Narratological theory, such as is discussed shortly, positively requires a wealth of detailed and local examples as part of the process of definition, and these are indeed to be found in the following pages. Other theories, which operate at a less schematic and more global level, lend themselves less well to point-by-point exemplification of this kind. As a result, I have found it expedient to provide larger and more extended examples in chapter 6 and 7 of this book. The patient (or not-so-patient) reader may therefore be encouraged to know that they will eventually be forthcoming. If this therefore means that, in a book which argues against excessive reliance upon empirical methods, and casts doubt upon teleology as a method of interpretation, I have now surreptitiously reintroduced both, then this is a price that I am cheerfully prepared to pay.

2 Structuralism and the science of narratives

Every culture that we know, or can possibly imagine, is perfused with narrative; indeed, the organization of the narratives and of the culture may have important features in common. Barthes (1966) speaks of narrative as 'a prodigious variety of genres, themselves distributed among different substances—as though any material were fit to receive man's stories' (p. 79). What he means by genre is easy enough to establish; he himself lists 'myth, legend, fable, tale, novella, epic, history, tragedy, drama, comedy, mime, painting ... stained glass windows, cinema, comics, news item, conversation' (p. 79) as actual or potential types of narrative. 'Substance' is perhaps an unfamiliar term to choose for the medium of transmission, but this is what Barthes intends by it, as he speaks of 'articulated language, spoken or written, fixed or moving images, gestures, and the ordered mixture of all these substances' (p. 79). Then, emboldened by these instances of cultural prodigality, he claims that 'narrative is international, transhistorical, transcultural; it is simply there, like like itself' (p. 79).

I incline towards caution at this point. Some form of narrative may indeed be detectable everywhere, but plotting the incidence of the various types may lead us to conclusions more interesting than mere intimations of universality. For example, we could draw up a simple matrix by plotting Barthes' 'genres' along one axis and his 'substances' along the other. We could then use this matrix in several ways. One would be to trace the transmutation of 'the same' narrative through various genres. For example, narrative prose by Isherwood describing prewar Berlin (*Goodbye to Berlin*) becomes first a play (*I am a Camera*), then a musical (*Cabaret*) and finally a film. In commonsense terms, this remains the same narrative throughout. However, not only are there changes of structure and emphasis, such as the role played by Sally Bowles in the narrative, but there are also quite different culturally mediated perceptions of the artefact. What degree of 'sameness' of narrative is there between *Old Possum's Book of Practical Cats*, light verse written by a serious and still respected poet, and *Cats*, a highly successful West End musical, for example?

But the other thing that we could do with the matrix, if we attached a date to each entry, would be to plot the rise and fall of genres through time. Typically, for example, entries under 'epic' would bear an earlier date than those under 'novella' or 'cinema'. Work such as this has led to various versions of cultural history, one of the more notable recent ones being that of Frye (1957).

But, just as there are difficulties in deciding what is 'the same' about a narrative repeated in various substances, so there is a problem in determining what the various genres themselves have in common. What, in other words, is the defining feature that all narratives share? Prince (1982) tries to illustrate the point by saying that

> Roses are red
> Violets are blue
> Sugar is sweet
> And so are you

is not a narrative, whereas 'John was very rich then he began to gamble and he became very poor' does constitute one. It isn't that the latter is a more interesting story, but rather that it starts by describing one state, and then identifies a change which brings about a second state. Barthes (1966) had earlier made something like the same point by saying that

> the mainspring of narrative is precisely the confusion of consecution and consequence, what comes *after* being read in narrative as what is *caused by*; in which case narrative would be a systematic application of the logical fallacy denounced by Scholasticism in the formula *post hoc, ergo propter hoc*. (p. 94)

This formula can roughly be translated as saying that if something comes after something then it happens on account of it.

Narrative is therefore a means of making sense of a series of events, real or imaginary, by imputing causal connections to them. In Prince's example above, for instance, it is worth noting that the text does not explicitly assert that the poverty was a product of the gambling, but it is safe to assume that most readers will make this inference.

There is therefore inbuilt, even in the purest and most text-oriented versions of narratology, a role for the reader that is in many ways constitutive; consider, for instance, the significance of the word 'read' in the Barthes quotation above. The same point emerges, even more explicitly, in Prince's concluding definition of narrativity:

> The narrativity of a text depends on the extent to which that text fulfils a reader's desire by representing oriented temporal wholes, involving some

sort of conflict, made up of discrete, specific and positive events, and meaningful in terms of a human project and a humanized universe. (p. 160)

Desire projected onto a universe in order to make it meaningful; this isn't the way in which the study of narrativity was originally conceived. Yet this desire is not formless and inchoate; there exists, so to speak, a grammar of desire. Just as the traditional project of grammarians was to analyse the constituent elements of a sentence and their different levels of integration and organization, so narratologists have always aimed to carry out the same process on narratives. The generally acknowledged founding father of twentieth-century narratology was Propp, who, (1928) tried to codify the ordinary reader's impression, when going through a corpus of Russian folk tales, 'Ah, here comes the one where ... again'. Propp systematized this perception by identifying events which could take place in a narrative, finding thirty-one of them in all, and terming them 'functions'. A function is defined not by *what* happens at that point in the text, but by *how* it interrelates to other functions within the narrative; whether, for instance, it is a step along the road, or the actual goal to be achieved. And just as ordinary grammars are characterized by rules of restriction (for example, in a given language an adjective must precede a noun if it occurs at all) so, in Propp, functions can only occur in a given order.

This tightly-structured grammar has been criticized in many ways, as founding works tend to be; narratologists often resemble characters in narratives in that they are torn between a passion for inheritance and fantasies in which they are the aboriginal inhabitants of their world—autochthonous, as anthropologists would call them. Propp's is a highly linear narrative analysis, and it has relatively little to say about the way in which functions combine in order to form higher level units of meaning. It is as though it is a grammar which describes parts of speech but can't say anything much about phrase structure. This search for a vertical, integrative structure to match the horizontal linear succession of narrative units is one that will come to predominate in the work of later narratologists.

But there is another criticism which can be made of Propp's work—or at least a limitation that can be traced back to the corpus on which it was based. If each tale ends with the shepherd marrying the princess, or the hero finding the pot of gold, then Propp may be right to say that these endings are functionally equivalent to each other, and the suggestion that they correspond to, and in some way enact, the desire of the Russian peasant for food (for which princess and gold are, in effect, metaphors) is a plausible one. Propp is offering a grammar of one of the most basic of desires. But this grammar cannot then cope with narratives which end in frustration and failure, except by classing them as narratologically ungrammatical. There is thus a loss of generalized explanatory force, but a gain in specific cultural applicability in such a method.

Later narratologists, however, have opted for generalized explanatory force as their greatest priority. Thus Greimas (1973) reduced the number of roles that might be played by a character in the course of a narrative to six (sender, object, receiver, helper, subject, opponent) and Bremond (1966) devised a system in which the potentiality of an event could result in either failure or success. A grammar which incorporates this perpetual bifurcation can cope with any number of possible twists and turns in the plot.

However, the most generally influential grammar of narrative was that of Barthes (1966) already referred to. Unlike the largely linear grammar of Propp, Barthes' model postulates various levels of integration, which I have attempted to represent in Figure 3. At the most basic level (which can be roughly compared with that of words in a conventional grammar of sentences) are to be found the minimal narrative units of the scheme. Barthes takes as his starting point Propp's and Bremond's notion of functions, but he subdivides these into two categories, which he terms nuclei and catalyzers. The words are intended to be self-descriptive, since nuclei are the irreducible, irreplaceable units of plot, whereas catalyzers have an auxiliary role, enabling nuclei to carry out their work. Using Bremond's system of nodal points in a narrative, at which something either will or will not take place, Barthes speaks of a nucleus as denoting an action which opens or continues or closes 'an alternative that is of direct consequence for the subsequent development of the story, in short, that it inaugurate(s) or conclude(s) an uncertainty' (p. 94). Catalyzers are much weaker functions in relation to the development of the

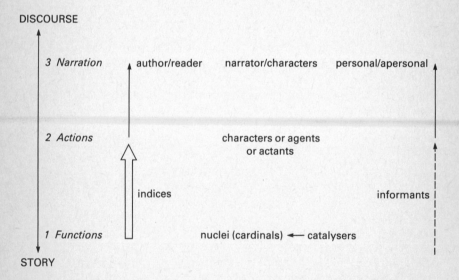

Figure 3   A representation of narrative levels and units as described by Barthes (1966)

plot, as they merely ' "fill in" the narrative space separating the hinge functions' (p. 93). As an example of a nucleus, Barthes offers the purchase of a revolver, which anticipates the moment at which it will be (or, alternatively, will not be) used. To illustrate what he sees as merely catalyzers, Barthes speaks of 'a host of trivial incidents or descriptions' such as ' "Bond moved towards the desk, picked up one of the receivers, put down his cigarette" etc.' (p. 94). For Barthes, the connection between these events is merely chronological, whereas the connection between the purchase and the use of a revolver is both chronological and logical—the use is an outcome of the purchase.

What is being said here seems very much in accordance with common-sense perceptions of how narrative functions. When people are asked to summarize a narrative they tend to pick out what Barthes calls the nuclei of what they read and to omit the catalyzers. Nevertheless, there are two questions that ought to be asked at this point. One is whether the difference between these two units is one of kind or of degree. Mostly, Barthes seems to consider that it is one of kind. But, in the examples of catalyzers that have just been given, it does seem that, formally at least, they possess much the same features as nuclei. When Bond moves towards the desk, he can either reach it or trip over the carpet; when he puts down a cigarette, it can either go out or start a fire, and so on. Both literature and life abound in examples of seemingly trivial incidents that have major consequences and, in each case, the importance that we attach to the incident is a retrospective process of evaluation and interpretation.

The other point that can be considered is whether there is any unit in narrative that is small enough to slip through the mesh of causal connections. Barthes himself makes the point that in verbal narrative (as compared with, for instance, film) there is no component present that has not been placed there by the author, so that, in this sense if in no other, the fabric consists of pure intentional meaning. Even something that seems meaningless (if, for instance, the hero walks down the street and notices a dog lying asleep on the pavement) can have the meaning of meaninglessness. It seems as though people are constitutionally incapable of treating anything in narrative as purely accidental or irrelevant.

In Barthes' view, a different type of connectedness is operating here—not the logical/chronological one of narrative flow, in which event produces event like billiard balls colliding on the table, but an interpersonal one in which the writer is signalling something to the reader. Whereas the onward march of nuclei belongs to the domain of the text, Barthes sees catalyzers as relating principally to the domain of discourse, in which they 'lay out areas of safety, rest, luxuries' (p. 95) between the risky high points of the narrative flow, allowing the reader to recover equanimity before the next crisis comes. The function that a catalytic passage has to fulfil is one that relates principally to the reader, since 'it accelerates, delays, gives fresh impetus to the discourse, it summarizes, anticipates and sometimes even leads astray' (p. 95). Using Jakobson's (1960) terminology, Barthes sees the catalyzer as having a phatic function, keeping open the channel between addresser and addressee.

I have used here both 'reader' and 'addressee' for what may prove to be not identical concepts, as was suggested in the first chapter, and I shall want to return to them, and to others that belong to the same cluster, later on. But first it is necessary to distinguish another dimension, other than that of straightforward narrative flow, along which, according to Barthes, information is transmitted. Whilst the reader is progressing through time and through the pages of the book, a whole new set of concepts is being built up, developed, modified, and occasionally reversed. If put into words, they might emerge as something like 'that man is attractive' or 'the organization he works for is a powerful one'. These notions are not purely personal and idiosyncratic ones, since most readers from the same culture would be likely to agree on them. Nevertheless, they usually cannot be ascribed in their entirety to one particular unit of text; however, they must have been generated by the text, or at least triggered off by it.

Barthes terms these triggers indices and, like nuclei and catalyzers, indices cannot be defined by their length or by their categorization by a sentence grammar, but only by what they do. In one of Barthes' examples, 'Bond picked up one of the four receivers', we are told that the fact that there are as many as four telephones on a desk indexes the large administrative machine of which he is a part, the notion that his actions serve to maintain order, and so on. It is important to point out, too, that whereas I located these ongoing, cumulative concepts in the reader's mind, Barthes, at least in this early essay, seems to want to give them something like the same objective analytic validity that 'noun' and 'verb' might have. Indeed he says that 'classes (of narrative unit) are to be determined without recourse to the substance of content (psychological substance for example), (pp. 91–2).

'Nucleus' and 'catalyzer' were strong and weak units respectively as far as horizontal narrative flow is concerned. 'Indices', by the same token, are strong vertical units in Barthes' analytical model, and there exist also weaker vertical units, which he terms informants. His definition of these is very cursory, but he does say that they serve 'to identify, to locate in time and space', that they bring 'ready-made knowledge', and that they 'embed fiction in the real world'. His example of an informant at this point is of a narrative unit that states the exact age of a character, and he implies that there is no great decoding needed to appreciate the significance of this information. Indices, in contrast, need working on, so that when you read that the moon can be seen half-hidden by thick billowing clouds you deduce that it is a stormy summer night, and go on to build up a picture of a heavy, anguish-laden atmosphere.

The final point to be made in describing this scheme is that, just as in a crossword a letter can figure in both 1 down and 7 across, so in Barthes' scheme a narrative unit can function both horizontally as an element in plot development, and vertically in indexing character or atmosphere. 'To drink a whisky (in an airport lounge) is an action which can act as a catalyzer to the (nuclear) notion of *waiting*, but it is also, and simultaneously, the indice of a certain atmosphere (modernity, relaxation, reminiscence, etc.), (pp. 96–7).

Events in the real world take place in unidirectional real time. Events in the simplest kind of realistic narrative fiction seek to mimic this and, when this fiction is read, the process of reading is of course a real-life event that takes place in real time. Barthes' analysis, however, moves away from both the real time of actual readings and the simulated time of the narrative structure, and ascends vertically to the higher levels of organization he has been mapping out. This higher level of organization, he emphasizes, is atemporal, and the point can best be illustrated in the following way. If I put three oranges on a table, and then take away one so that two are left, that constitutes a sequence of events in real time. The little narrative in my previous sentence tried to simulate a real-life sequence of events. However, the formula $3-1=2$ in no way mimics a temporal sequence, but instead describes a set of relationships between different numerical values. Barthes sees the integrative relationships of narrative structure as much more akin to the mathematical formula than to the cumulative impressions that may be built up in a reader's mind during the reading of a narrative. The references to the reader's role, tentatively extended during the course of the essay, are soon withdrawn and do not reappear until some years later.

This atemporal abstraction is important because it lines Barthes up with a number of other theorists in different areas. For instance, some statements about transformational rules in a Chomskyan grammar would apply to the vertical movement in Barthes' scheme, and Chomsky's deep structure is also atemporal. And just as, at a deep structural level, the subject of the sentence 'The dog bit the policeman' is identical to the agent in 'The policeman was bitten by the dog', so Barthes' description of narrative structure is trying to get beyond the merely commonsense level of realist, referential writing, and identify units that can only be perceived by an analytic approach.

In doing so, he is being considerably influenced by the work of the anthropologist Lévi-Strauss (1955), whose analysis of myths claimed that their true significance only emerged when their underlying elements were being seen in relation to each other. A typical formulation has the look of something like '*a* is to *b* as *c* is to *d*', as in his account of the Oedipus myths: some blood relations are overstressed (as in incest); some are understressed (as when members of a family kill one another); some elements of narrative have figures denying that they are earthborn (as when Oedipus kills the Sphinx); some show irrefutable evidence of an earthborn origin (as with Oedipus's swollen foot). For Lévi-Strauss the meaning of the myth emerges when these elements are combined: 'the overrating of blood relations is to the underrating of blood relations as the attempt to escape autochthony is to the impossibility to succeed in it'. This example can be difficult to follow, because it refers to some of the lesser-known parts of the Oedipus story, but the shape of his logic is clear enough to see. It is important, too, to notice that this decoding takes place in at least two ways and at two different levels. An anthropologist is able to proceed consciously and to deploy mathematical logic as an interpretative tool, but this kind of analysis is only undertaken in the first place because a society is deploying myth in this way to define and transmit its understandings of the workings of the universe and the consequences this produces for human action.

But which 'society' are we talking about here? At first glance the answer would seem to be pre-classical Greece, but Lévi-Strauss casts his net wider than this, and insists that all interpretations of the Oedipus myth, including, for instance, Freud's, become superimposable for the anthropologist-as-narratologist to study. This recalls the transhistoricity that Barthes was ascribing to narrative. But Barthes, even in the same essay, could be more cautious than this. He writes that, above the first level of narrative flow and the second of actants, there is to be found a third level of narration itself, which is concerned with the relation between the narrator and the character, with the omniscience or the limited point of view of the narrating in relation to what is being narrated—in a word, with the discourse of the work. To go outside this, says Barthes, is to transgress the boundaries of the work and to become involved in other systems, social, economic, ideological, or whatever. 'Just as linguistics stops at the sentence, so narrative analysis stops at discourse—from there it is necessary to shift to another semiotics' (pp. 115–6). This is a curious hybrid comment, because it acknowledges that there are other legitimate domains of investigation (here he seems to differ from the implications of Lévi-Strauss's approach) but, if they are to be analysed by semiotics, they are susceptible to very much the same kind of investigation that narratives are; *autre pays*, but not *autres moeurs*.

This confidence that semiotic method was adequate for the resolution of any type of problem in any domain is characteristic of structuralism at the highest and most confident point in its development. Most later theories, however much they may differ among themselves, agree in assuming that the interpretation of social processes requires other and different disciplines.

But, in discussing the interplay between discourse and society, as Barthes uses these two terms, I have rather slipped past the definition of what discourse is held to be. This is partly in imitation of Barthes himself, whose account of the upper end of his narrative model is a lot thinner than that of the bottom. So let me try to remedy this omission by reverting to a point I made earlier, when I quoted Barthes as saying that catalyzers 'lay out areas of safety, rest, luxuries' between the narrative crunch points of nuclei. But rest and recuperation are not the only responses possible during these forty-eight hour leaves from narrative duty. If the first nucleus consists of the firing of a gun, and the second of the collapse of a victim on the floor, then these events, had they happened in real time, would have been virtually instantaneous. In narrative, however, they can be separated by any number of catalyzers, and the effect of these on the reader is to increase tension and suspense in rough proportion to their number and in positive correlation to their perceived irrelevance. This is what Barthes means by saying that catalyzers reinforce contact with the reader; they also, in instances such as this, serve as a reminder that a narrative is not just a simple mimesis of real or imaginary events, but an act of interchange with the reader which self-consciously reveals its own artificiality.

A more detailed examination of narrative structures of this kind was undertaken by Genette in his *Narrative Discourse* (1972). In this he explores the often very complex relationships between the ordering of events in the course of a narrative and the order in which they would have occurred had they been real. In simple folk-tales, for example, the narrative may be as uncomplicated and unilinear as the incidents that are being related, and this has sometimes led commentators to suggest that this is a feature of oral literature in general, deriving perhaps from a lack of psychological capability to process complex narratives without visual prompting. To say this, though, is to ignore the often highly complex narrative structure of many oral epics. But let us look instead at a novel that has already been mentioned in this book, and one that is not usually thought of as structurally complex—Mark Twain's *The Adventures of Tom Sawyer* (1876). The sequence in which Tom and Becky get lost in the caves is handled as follows.

A day trip by steamer to the caves is organized. Becky then agrees with her mother that she will spend the night with her friend Suzy Harper. Secretly she agrees with Tom to go to Widow Douglas's instead. All the day trippers spend too long in the caves, and have to race to catch the steamer home. Huck watches the steamer return. The narrative then follows Huck as he stalks Injun Joe, prevents his intended attack on Widow Douglas, and consequently is fêted by the townsfolk. They then go to church, where Mrs Thatcher and Tom's Aunt Polly discover that Becky and Tom are missing, and must therefore be in the caves still. A search is conducted over the following three days, but without result. The next chapter (32) begins with the words 'Now to return to Tom and Becky's share in the picnic' (p. 173) and follows their fruitless efforts to discover a way out, in the course of which Tom Sawyer sights, and hides from, Injun Joe. After some while 'Tom believed it must be Wednesday or Thursday, or even Friday or Saturday, now, and that the search had been given over' (p. 181). Becky settles down to die, while Tom goes exploring once more.

Chapter 33 then begins with the words 'Tuesday afternoon came', and says that most searchers have given up, and public prayers have been said. The opening paragraph, though summarizing events that have already happened, specifies that time moves on to Tuesday night. Then, in the second paragraph, bells are rung, and people shout that the pair have been found. Tom lies on a sofa in the Thatchers' house recounting how he discovered a way out.

As all good cinemagoers know, what we have had here is an extended flashback—'Meanwhile back at the ranch . . .' In Genette this goes by the more dignified and technical title of analepsis. There is good reason for this formality, since even a fairly conventional narrative can deploy more analepsis than most avant-garde films. Thus, while the whole of Chapter 32 is analeptic, so is a sentence in Chapter 33, such as 'Public prayers had been offered up for them'. Examples like this abound; what is more difficult to discover is any example of prolepsis—the 'flash-forward'. The nearest we come to it is when we hear of Becky in the cave that 'She said she would wait, now, where she was, and die—it would not be long', but, since this is indirect speech, it is not something vouched for by the narrative.

The examples of analepsis I quoted above related in each case to the subject under discussion and so would be classed by Genette as homo-diegetic or relating to the same story. An analepsis that relates to some other character or theme would be classed as heterodiegetic, and again forms no part of Twain's method at this point. However, it is worth noticing how complicated the use of homodiegetic analepsis can be here. Chapter 33 ends with Tom's realization that the doors of the cave have been sealed, a fortnight has passed, and Injun Joe is trapped inside. In Chapter 34 the body is discovered, and an extensive analepsis recounts what Injun Joe had done during his last days: hacking at the cave door, eating bats, catching the drips from a stalactite. But then an analepsis within an analepsis suddenly extends the timescale much further:

> That drop was falling when the pyramids were new; when Troy fell; when the foundations of Rome were laid; when Christ was crucified; when the Conqueror created the British Empire; when Columbus sailed; when the massacre at Lexington was 'news'. It is falling now; it will still be falling when all these things shall have sunk down the afternoon of history . . .
>
> (p. 185)

What started as analepsis progresses to become the first satisfactory prolepsis we have found. Moreover, since they manifestly go beyond the timescale of the narrative as a whole, the analepsis and prolepsis here are examples of what Genette calls external anachrony, rather than the internal kind, which falls within the timespan of the main narrative. Then, to round the paragraph off, a less ambitious external prolepsis occurs:

> It is many and many a year since the hapless half-breed scooped out the stone to catch the priceless drops, but to this day the tourist stares longest at that pathetic stone and that slow dropping water when he comes to see the wonders of McDougal's cave.

So far I have been illustrating what Genette has to say about order within narrative. However, a piece of writing like the one we are examining here also illustrates the way in which the pace of narrative can vary. I use 'pace' in a conventional sense here, but of course it is a recognized fiction in itself, since no two readings of the same story progress at exactly the same speed. The term is usually used in recognition of the fact that the ratio of words of text to units of narrated time is not constant. It comes nearest to being constant in passages of dialogue, but the account of the children's recovery after their ordeal—'They were bedridden all of Wednesday and Thursday'—is clearly running faster than any dialogue would. However, even more extreme examples occur in the earlier passage where Huck has been tailing Injun Joe. He goes for help to an old Welshman.

> 'By George, he *has* got something to tell, or he wouldn't act so!' exclaimed the old man. 'Out with it, and nobody here'll ever tell, lad.' Three minutes later the old man and his sons, well armed, were up the hill ... [Huck follows them and hears a bang and a cry.]
> He sprang away and sped down the hill as fast as his legs could carry him.

Chapter 31 follows straight on, and opens with:

> As the earliest suspicion of dawn appeared on Sunday morning, Huck came groping up the hill and rapped gently at the old Welshman's door.

In the first instance we know that three minutes have elapsed, and in the second we conjecture several hours. What we have here are examples of ellipsis, the extreme form of narrative acceleration. Technically, indeed, this represents greater acceleration than the passage about the water-drops, since, though the latter spanned millennia, it took some sixty words to do so, whereas ellipsis takes none at all.

The polar opposite to this kind of acceleration is the deceleration that comes when a narrative 'stands still' to describe a scene. My first impulse here was to illustrate the point with a passage providing a description of the cave, until I realized that this is all mediated through the perceptions of the visitors, and so retains a narrative pace. 'In one place they found a spacious cavern ... they walked all about it' (p. 174). What I was looking for was a passage like 'The caves are readily described. A tunnel eight feet long, five feet high, three feet wide, leads to a circular chamber about twenty feet in diameter. This arrangement occurs again and again throughout the group of hills', but I am cheating here, because this particular passage continues 'and this is all, this is a Marabar cave' (Forster, 1924, p. 130). Here, in *A Passage to India*, Forster's narrative strategies are, throughout, distinctly different.

The final set of Genette's categories that I want to introduce at this point is that relating to frequency in narrative. The simplest and most common kind, singulative, consists of the telling once what is supposed to have happened once. Reverting to *Tom Sawyer* for examples, we can take a sentence like 'The old Welshman came home towards daylight' (p. 172), but most sentences from a book such as this would serve as well.

A less frequent device is iterative narration, in which the narrative records once what may be considered to have happened several times. A good deal of the account of the search for the children is presented in this way, as in a sentence like 'Judge Thatcher sent messages of hope and encouragement from the cave' (p. 172), where we may assume that, as a rational and capable man, he did not send them all together at one time.

But the earlier passage, which relates how the picnic party explored the caves, manifests a more complex and subtler mixture of singulative and iterative narration. It begins with 'By and by somebody shouted: "Who's ready for the cave?"' (p. 160) and moves on to sentences like 'The moment a candle was lighted, there was a general rush upon the owner of it'; it then reverts to 'By and by the procession went filing down the steep descent of the main avenue' before becoming iterative again with 'Every few steps, other lofty and still narrower crevices branched from it', and so on with a skilfully controlled confusion until a concluding iterative passage, 'By and by, one group after another came straggling back to the mouth of the cave' succeeds in implying, without ever stating, that the cave is now empty.

The third of Genette's categories of frequency is the repetitive, which, as the name suggests, is the opposite of the iterative in that it states several times what may be considered to have happened once. From the account I have given, you would not expect to find it frequently deployed here, since it is not a device that typically contributes to the production of the kind of narrative tension that *Tom Sawyer* demonstrates. Nevertheless there are examples to be found, and they occur chiefly at the beginning of Chapter 32, where the narrative reverts to Tom's and Becky's adventures in the cave after having described the search for them. In the first paragraph there are sentences such as 'They tripped along the murky aisles with the rest of the company' and 'Presently the hide-and-seek frolicking began' which explicitly identify the children's actions with those of the other trippers—actions that were already described at an earlier point in the story.

Does any of this matter? Like so much literary theory, it teeters along a thin borderline between stating the obvious and marshalling a complex of terms and concepts that seem to have little to do with human experience. Indeed, the worst possible outcome would be to provide a justification for a series of worksheets in which pupils were required to find three examples of iterative narrative on page 94. In addition we have the further complication that a lot of narrative theory, such as that of Barthes discussed earlier, belongs to a high and confident phase of structuralism that most scholars no longer subscribe to; indeed, Barthes himself, as we shall later see, modified his position quite radically in respect of most of the issues we have been looking at.

Nevertheless, I think that there are good pedagogical reasons for teachers to engage with some of the concepts and methods of narratology. To begin with, the narrative strategies of a text must be considered a significant feature of its readability. At what age, for instance, can a child first cope with iterative or repetitive narrative? To what degree is skill in coping a matter of maturation, or a product of lived experience, or does exposure to these devices in texts selected for reading determine the level of competence? These are questions which require empirical investigation, but such investigation can only be carried out on the basis of a prior knowledge of narratological devices.

Secondly, the ability to process and understand text cannot be divorced from the perceived relevance of the text to the reader. It is a reasonable speculation, for instance, that Twain's passage dwelling on the development of the stalactite through millennia has bored many younger readers who have not actually skipped it. Intuitively, many teachers over the years must have devised their own means of coping with this: encouraging pupils to skip, encouraging them to develop their own ideas of large units of time, or whatever. In the context of the school curriculum many strategies are possible, including an attempt to correct Twain's error in supposing William the Conqueror to be in some significant sense the father of the British Empire. Nevertheless, in the context of developing an understanding of the book, a teacher's efforts must focus on enabling pupils to grasp the relevance of this extradiegetic material, in seeing that to a human mind part of the horror of a death in a cave is the contrast between the extreme mutability of flesh and the relative immutability of rock and water. This is a theme that is signalled in Tom's and Becky's comments and actions, but developed explicitly for the first time in this passage. It is, in Barthes' use of the term, an aspect of the discourse; it is something that operates at the third and highest level of narrative structure.

But various other aspects of Barthes' model can also be usefully drawn on in connection with this passage of narrative. I have tried in summary to show how Twain produced an inter-cut or intercalated narrative sequence, in which not only do we jump from the villagers to the children, but we have also, so to speak, a series of snapshot representations of the last days of Injun Joe. And, at every point where the two narrative threads intersect, Injun Joe is the loser, and the acute reader ought to be able to spot the loss before it happens. In some cases the interval is short: between the statement by Judge Thatcher that he has had the door to the cave sealed up and the statement that Injun Joe has been killed by this action there is a space of seven lines. The nucleus that was constituted by the first act inevitably brings about the second, just as the purchase of a gun signals its eventual use. But these two nuclei are separated by a series of positively exemplary catalyzers, in which Tom turns white, water is called for, water is brought, water is thrown in Tom's face. Dangerous though it is to speculate about an author's motives, it does seem very likely that these events are placed here chiefly in order to provide 'thinking time' for the reader, during which the dreadful consequences can be deduced. They are 'moments of rest', but of a particularly vertiginous kind.

Other nuclei have much longer intervals between them. Injun Joe's treasure, the search for which occupies much of the book, is removed to a place of safety in Chapter 27, and it is not until Chapter 34 that this place is discovered to be the cave itself. Yet Injun Joe's brief appearance in the cave may be taken as a clue in this quest, a nucleus placed halfway between the problem and its resolution. Barthes stresses that his terminology is provisional and arbitrary, and he would have been the last to object to a teaching strategy which invited pupils to concentrate on these 'important points' in a narrative and draw conclusions about them.

Judge Thatcher, though an important figure in the book, is a shadowy one, accorded virtually no direct speech and little description. Yet it is his work, and his exercise of parental authority, which cause Becky to appear in the village, and to disappear from time to time. His authority extends further than this, however: his organizing of the search seems to stem as much from his role in the community as from his role as a parent, and, of the various indices to his character and status that the text provides, the sealing-up of the cave is perhaps the clearest. A practical teaching strategy therefore would be to devise a series of questions about the standing of the Judge within the community (a series which would probably produce a high degree of intersubjective agreement) and then to ask for reasons for these answers. There is no call to name these reasons indices, but that is what they undoubtedly are.

There is, though, a further reason to work upwards from the first level of narrative flow to the second of narrated character, and that is that it provides us with access to the third level of discourse—the relationship between the narration and that which is being narrated. The following passage occurs in the thirty-sixth and final chapter:

> Judge Thatcher hoped to see Tom a great lawyer or a great soldier some day. He said he meant to look to it that Tom should be admitted to the National Military Academy, and afterwards trained in the best law-school in the country, in order that he might be ready for either career, or both.

Here again these brief comments serve as indices of the Judge's power, a power that has also just been illustrated by the trusteeship that he exercises over Tom's half of the treasure. But, at the level of discourse, we seem to be seeing these career options ratified as desirable, as the happy ending that is almost implicit in the single sheet that we realize is all that is left for us to read. However, the discourse is more complex that this, because not only does Tom continue with his playful identification with the role of robber (the role in which Injun Joe actually accrued the capital in the first place) but also, and much more radically, we have Huck's profound unease at the life of respectability which his newfound wealth has created for him. Though his actual opting-out (he goes back, until persuaded otherwise, to live in his old empty barrel) is contained within the fantasy-robbing that Tom persuades him to accept as an occasional alternative, its force, ratified by the depiction of all the earlier scenes of idyllic childhood freedom, is enough to complicate the ending of the novel considerably.

A traditional literary critic at this point would have recourse to a number of convenient terms. Ambiguity would be one, and another, complexity, I have already caught myself using. There would also be discussion of moral growth, of the vices of a rigid and utilitarian civilization, and of the countervailing values of spontaneity and the Wordsworthian innocence of childhood. It is not possible, in any simple and straightforward way, to say that all of this is wrong. Some elements of it undoubtedly can be traced, by the kinds of approaches I have outlined, upwards through the various textual levels, and it may be possible to argue that they are there in that case as objective features of the text. Other aspects of this commentary may indeed be seen as more purely ideological, as a comforting myth of a lost childhood Eden that serves to valorize a retreat from the problems of current life. Perhaps, though, we should follow Lévi-Strauss's example at this point, and treat these ideological interpretations as part of the data that have to be examined.

What does seem likely, though, is that any discussion of the novel as a whole that pays no attention to the level of discourse generated by the processes of the text will remain stuck at a fairly rudimentary stage. I would suggest, therefore, that any teacher approaching this text, and with virtually any set of pupils in mind, has of necessity to come to grips with the level of discourse and the devices by which it is generated. Is Tom happier at the end than at the beginning? Is Huck? Which would you rather be? Would others agree with you? Is too much respectability a bad thing? Does the freedom to do as you please pose any problems? These are not, in themselves, new questions, and it would be naïve to pretend that they lack any ideological colouring themselves. But a study of the functioning of narrative processes may help teachers to formulate them better, and it should certainly provide the scope to ratify their conclusions by a more objective examination of the text than would otherwise have been possible.

3 Putting the reader in her place

In the first chapter of this book I cited Jakobson's model of a speech event, in which, on the central axis, there were to be found just three items which formed a sequence: addresser, message, and addressee. In the second chapter I indicated that there might be some problems with the last of those three terms when it came to applying them to a work of literature. Does an addressee consist of the kind of readership that the writer originally had in mind? Or does it consist of the actual reader every time a book is 'consumed' at any point in the future? Comparisons with more conventional speech events are of limited help here. If I phone my grandmother then she is my intended addressee, and anyone else who hears what I am saying on a crossed line is simply an intruder. If I read a love letter addressed to my sister then she remains the addressee despite that the fact that I am the reader, and any attempt on my part to apply the pronoun 'you' in text to myself is likely to lead to some very curious outcomes. Yet surely the reader of a novel has a status other than that of a snooper or eavesdropper? Let us take one further case, that of a writer of a diary. Who is the addressee here? In the first instance, presumably, the writer herself, who doubles this role with the one of addresser. Yet, unless she all the while intends that the book should be burnt after her death, she is in some sense assuming that there will be some other addressee, whether known to her or not. But, whoever is the intended reader of the diary, that person is unlikely to be named as such in the text; indeed, in the 'Dear Diary' approach, we have the paradox of the contact becoming the ostensible addressee! By a somewhat similar process, literary texts can create ostensible readers who are just as fictional as the characters in a story. Just as a novel can be ostensibly told by a fictional narrator, so it can be told to a fictional narratee. In some instances the narrator/narratee compact forms the framework for the entire narrative, as in those Joseph

Conrad novels that are related by Marlow. In other instances the narratee seems to slide in and out of existence. I am not actually going to claim that Conrad is in general exceeded in textual subtlety by Jerome K. Jerome, but I should like to consider the following passages from *Three Men in a Boat* (1889).

> If you were to stand at night by the seashore with Harris, and say 'Hark, do you not hear? Is it but the mermaids singing deep below the waving waters; or sad spirits, chanting dirges for white corpses, held by seaweed?'
> Harris would take you firmly by the arm, and say:
>   'I know what it is, old man; you've got a chill.'   (pp. 18–19)

Here the pronoun 'you' could be said to substitute for the impersonal pronoun 'one', but the device is used so persistently throughout the book that it comes to seem more like a kindly friend talking to an amnesiac; the narratee is virtually the fourth man in the boat.

> Throw the lumber over, man! Let your boat of life be light, packed with only what you need ... You will have time to think as well as to work. Time to drink in life's sunshine—time to listen to the Aeolian music that the wind of God draws from the human heart-strings around us—time to— I beg your pardon, really. I quite forgot.   (p. 27)

There can be no question here of an impersonal usage; the narratee is being both hectored at and apologized to. Throughout the narrative the sudden presence or absence of a more or less concretized narratee (for most of the text consists of conventional first-person narrative interspersed with direct speech) is deeply bound up with changes in narrating style, from conversational to self-consciously inflated, and in many respects the narratee is treated as a normative figure by the narrator.

My use of the terms 'narrator' and 'narratee' in the above is taken from Booth (1961). Narratological tradition also offers us, in addition to the figure of the narratee, the concept of the implied reader, a concept particularly associated with the work of Iser, discussed later in this chapter. This figure of the implied reader has much in common with the readership envisaged by the author, but is by no means identical. In *Three Men in a Boat* the narratee, as we have seen, is practically an extra member of the crew. The implied reader would have much in common with him: young, male, lower-middle class, affable—this is the sort of person that the book appears to be directed towards. Yet the actual audience that Jerome was after would have included women, older people, and members of other social classes to a considerable degree.

Let me offer another example. David Lodge's novel *Changing Places* (1975), an account of an Anglo-American academic exchange, begins as a third-person narrative, and then, halfway through, changes to become an epistolary novel in which the characters exchange air-mail letters. Once this happens, we have a series of narratees, each of whom is the person to whom each letter is addressed. Later still the novel become a series of press-cuttings, press releases, students' union resolutions, and small ads, so that not only does the narrator change more frequently but it also becomes more difficult to specify who the narratee is in each case; usually the best we can do is to say 'the readership of a fictitious West Midlands newspaper' or some such formulation. The final 'chapter' is written in the form of a filmscript, and, like the opening third-person narrative, has no obvious narratee at all. Yet there is an implied reader running through all of this. In the first chapter the British academic meets on the plane an erstwhile student, Boon. The lecturer has been to the USA before, and assumes his companion has not.

> And for once he will have the advantage of Boon, in his previous experience of America. Boon will be eager for advice and information: about looking left first when crossing the road, for example.   (p. 37)

The effect of this passage is lost unless the reader assumes he is intended to know that traffic in the USA drives on the right, and to know also that this fact is widely known. Even if the reader for some reason does not know this fact he will realize at this point that he is expected to behave as if he had known it all along, and to judge that the lecturer's behaviour is somewhat patronizing. In other words, the actual (uninformed) reader will place himself in the position of the (well-informed) implied reader—a role that has been created by the book just as much as any of its characters have been. And, unlike the succession of narratees that occur in the book, this implied reader remains constant from beginning to end, with very much the same sort of demands, in terms of knowledge, moral values, and so on, remaining constant throughout.

It has always seemed to me that those who wish to argue that a particular book exercises a corrupting effect on its readership would do best to train their fire, not on the events that are narrated, but on the textual strategies that are involved in creating the implied reader. For instance, an ardent teetotaller who had studied some narratology would do well to pick out, not the scenes in which the rowers are depicted drinking in *Three Men in a Boat*, but the kind of implied reader who has a deep and detailed knowledge of Thamesside public houses. At a somewhat different level, the insidiousness of the question 'Have you stopped beating your wife yet?' lies in its creation of an implied figure for whom wife-beating is a habitual activity. In this trick question the challenge is blatant enough for the hearer to reject the role, but in much racist or sexist literature this may not be the case.

Where the value-system associated with the implied reader of a particular book is blatantly offensive, any teacher can attempt to do one of two things. One, of course, would be not to teach the book at all. The other would be to attempt a purely symptomatic reading, pointing out the devices by which the implied reader is created in order to objectivize and criticize this figure. Such a strategy entails a calculated risk, though, since the implied reader may be more attractive to the pupils than any alternative that the teacher can offer. In such a case textual strategies will prove stronger than teaching ones.

Not all implied readers, in any case, will be consensually defined as objectionable. Not everyone, for instance, will be inclined to feel that there is too much wrong with the conservative, spiritual, idealistic implied reader of George Herbert's poetry, or with the reformist, earnest, knowledgeable and slightly world-weary figure indicated by George Eliot's *Middlemarch*. Yet, for some radical critics, this combination of quietism and pessimism is deeply corrupting, and a typical outcome of a typical education in the literary Great Tradition.

In the examples I have used up to this point I have been assuming, for the sake of the discussion, that it is possible to specify with some certainty the characteristics of the implied reader as determined by any particular text. In practice, of course, such certainty cannot always be attained—or, if it can, we may be wise to question the grounds of our assumptions. An ironic narrative, for instance, frequently works by leaving the actual reader in some doubt about the features of the implied reader. In many cases these doubts can be resolved, but in others the solution, for historical or other reasons, is irretrievable. No amount of literary study and training will settle the question of whether the warfaring of Chaucer's Knight in *The Canterbury Tales* is to be seen by the implied reader as chivalrically honourable or humanly deplorable. Part of the trouble here can be traced back to the code (are we dealing with chivalric romance or aren't we?) but, more important perhaps, we have restricted access to the context, which itself would have indicated the degree of respect in which chivalric romance was held.

The conclusion I am pointing towards is that not only do literary texts have histories, but the meanings of literary texts have histories as well. To some people this may seem no more than a statement of the obvious, but to others it is a deeply threatening statement. For them, if meaning cannot be held constant across time, it then becomes impossible to ascribe permanent moral or aesthetic value to a particular text. How can a work of literature contribute to human well-being if at one time it casts a chivalric glamour over warfare, and at another it debunks and savages the whole process? Various strategies become possible at this point. One, an entirely respectable and well-established one, is to conduct literary or historical research into the question. For instance, if it can be shown that Chaucer's work resembles a number of others that are unambiguously pro- or anti-warfaring, then a degree of probability can be established that the relevant passage of *The General Prologue* is setting out the same specifications for its implied hearers/readers. Or, if it could be shown that a war had been about to break out, and that Chaucer had spent a spell in the Tower for opposing it, then that would constitute another category of proof.

But there are other strategies that are possible as well. One is to transfer the ambiguity from the code or the context to the message itself. If the text can be seen as both romanticizing and deploring carnage, then perhaps the implied reader is a more complex, more mature, more integrated and generally admirable character than the crypto-pacifist or the fourteenth-century militarist we have been considering so far? Perhaps exposure to texts that generate such a figure is therefore after all a morally beneficial process, producing citizens who will ponder issues of peace and war with the benefit of a sensibility refined by exposure to literature? This is the way that the case has often been argued, and elements of the argument can be traced back both to American 'New Criticism' of the postwar years, and to Leavisite precept, and practice, of the same period. A debased version of the argument, indeed, would hold that the more ambiguous the stance of the text, the more beneficial its effect on the reader, producing such a morally rounded character that she would be most unlikely ever to interrupt her profound ruminations with any form of civic action at all.

Another, and very different, type of approach consists of an attempt to see what sort of construction of meaning has been achieved by actual readers at different periods of history. Naturally enough, data for this kind of investigation is not always available, but in some cases there is enough to state with some degree of precision what different categories of reader made of particular texts. The kind of thing I have in mind here is what Mayhew (in 1851) managed to do by asking real-life Victorian pick-pockets their opinion of Dickens's *Oliver Twist* (1838). If enough samples of this kind can be obtained, and over a sufficient period of time, then some kind of demographic account of patterns of reader response becomes possible.

It is also possible to reincorporate this kind of demographic data into the figure of the implied reader once more. This is the kind of process that I take to be going on when Riffaterre (1966) speaks of the category of superreader, a protean figure rather than a Nietzschean one as he defines the term. In the essay I have in mind, as in his method more generally, Riffaterre is constructing an amalgam of all possible known readers of a particular text, in this case a sonnet by Baudelaire that had been analyzed by Jakobson and Lévi-Strauss. As opposed to the more purely message-centred techniques deployed by these two, Riffaterre is setting up for consideration an amalgam of responses by Baudelaire himself, by other French writers of the period, by various translators of the poem, by various current analysts, including the ones he is arguing against, by philologists and others, and by 'students of mine and other souls whom fate has thrown in my way' (p. 38). But, once such a hydra-headed monster has been created, I am not sure what use it will actually be to anybody—unless, like hydras in classical myth, it can be set to guarding treasure, which in this case consists of the purity and integrity of textual interpretation. Riffaterre's approach consists of recognizing that readings of texts are historically and culturally variable, but it does so only in order to produce a normative composite figure who can be used to eliminate the freaks and foibles of individual interpretation. Thus, though he is ostensibly examining the role of the reader, Riffaterre is in reality acting as a good paid-up structuralist in reasserting the primacy of the text.

Many other ostensibly reader-oriented approaches to literary theory share this feature of drawing back at the moment of commitment, of hesitating to commit themselves to the anarchy of awarding equal validity to each and every reading of a given text. But this anarchy need not prove, on closer inspection, to be anarchy at all; rather, it may be that patterns and coherences emerge when actual readings are examined and compared. However, the reasons for these patterns and coherences may have to be sought elsewhere than in the text itself. Perhaps, to text-oriented theorists, this may be the greatest threat of all.

Some of these features will be examined later in this book in considerations of the ways in which code and context contribute to the generation of meaning. But, for the present, let us continue to look at some more of the ways in which addressees contribute to the production of meaning every time a book is read. One, paradoxically enough, is locked into the very central notions of Russian formalism, which is usually, and not without reason, seen as an extremely text-centred approach to the study of literature. For the formalists the essence of literariness consisted of a form of deviation, a defamiliarization, in which accepted norms are transgressed. This deliberate breaking of the rules—this departure from the code—served to remind the reader that what was being read was literature. This was what Jakobson meant by describing literature as a process of focusing upon the message.

But defamiliarization can only go on working for so long. After a time the deviation from the norm itself comes to be read as a new norm; what was once an innovation has lost its power to shock and surprise. An example of this would be the 'indirect free style' of narration that Flaubert adopted in *Madame Bovary* (1857). Sufficiently novel at that time to produce a radical bewilderment amongst its audience (charges of immorality against Flaubert arose from a confusion over what was being said by the author, what by the narrator, and what thought by the principal character) this form of narration was later to become the standard form of the French novel, against which further deviations had to operate. But it only became the standard form because it was perceived as such, so that ultimately the criterion of what is familiar and what not has to rest with the actual readers of a work.

In certain ways this criterion of defamiliarization within formalist theory can be paralleled by the term 'horizon of expectations' as it is found in the rather different tradition of reception theory, and, in particular, in the work of Jauss (1970). As a term it does not lack ambiguity, since it picks up and focuses several aspects of the study of audience response.

When a reader opens a book he does so with a set of expectations that have already been brought to bear before a single word has been read. Different things are looked for from a novel than from a telephone directory or a travel brochure. Partly this has to do with the services that are to be provided by the different forms of reading matter: the railway traveller will read a guidebook for information, but a thriller for entertainment, for example. But partly it is to do with conventions, norms, genre characteristics that are more internal to the work in question. Imagine a public library-user examining a shelf of Tudor history, pulling off books at random to look at them. If we suppose that a novel set in Tudor England has been mistakenly placed on this shelf, then the opening of this book will undoubtedly cause some surprise. But the surprise will probably be only temporary; the library-user will quickly realize what has happened, and adjust her expectations accordingly, so that she is able to respond to and evaluate the work in question in a way that other library-users would consider appropriate. There is, therefore, a shared agreement, within the society in question, as to what constitutes a novel and what a history book. Moreover, even if two readers might differ as to how highly they regarded a particular novel, they might in all probability agree on what it was 'trying to do', and how far this was typical or otherwise of writing of this kind.

The amount of agreement of this kind that exists can be overstated; it will probably not hold for the other side of the world, and possibly may not for someone a few streets away. What can be even more confidently stated, though, is that it does not hold good across time. The Tudor novel would presumably greatly puzzle a magically resuscitated Shakespeare, for example. Partly this would be because prose fiction in English of a type we would recognize as the proto-novel was only just beginning in his lifetime; partly it would relate to the fact that different considerations governed the depiction of historical characters during the epoch in which he was writing. Most of us in idle moments must have toyed with fantastic conjunctures of different kinds: speculations such as 'What would Jane Austen have made of *Finnegan's Wake*?' Fancies such as these are prompted not just by some naïve assumption that James Joyce must be a lot cleverer than Jane Austen because he had the privilege of living in a time nearer to our own, but by the realization that norms and expectations have changed with the passage of years.

It is towards these norms and expectations that the phrase 'horizon of expectations' is pointing, and the effect that Jauss is seeking to bring off is to combine reference to the general norms and understandings of society at large with reference to the prevailing expectations of what a novel, a poem or a play should be like. In other words, the definition is both extrinsic and intrinsic to literature as an institution within society. This is a deliberate amalgam on Jauss's part, and not some accidental confusion that he has perpetrated. For him an unqualified reliance on general social norms would be a reductive form of sociologism, and a pure reliance on individual interpretation would be the start of a slippery slope downwards to solipsism and anarchy.

It also follows from these assumptions that the past—or at least the past of literary understandings—is in certain senses retrievable and knowable.

When literary works are first published they are interpreted according to the standards and prevailing understandings of those times. This initial interpretation then becomes part of the data that is presented to subsequent readers, along with the text itself. There must be relatively few people, seeing or reading *Romeo and Juliet* for the first time, who do not already 'know' that it is a tragedy of two young lovers in which the phrase 'Wherefore art thou, Romeo?' will appear at some point. When they actually experience the work for themselves, though, they will be struck by whatever features of it relate most strongly to their perceptions of how things are. It may be, for instance, that they will read it as a text dealing with the issues of teenage rebellion. This last term, which has only gained any currency in the last forty or so years, is emphatically not one that would have formed part of the horizon of understanding of Shakespeare and his contemporaries, yet is a feature of current readings, and so can legitimately be added to other concepts (such as that of the validity of dynastic marriages) which we, as readers, have inherited from previous generations of readers of this particular text.

It follows from all this that literary works which have an extensive history of being 'received' during different epochs are likely, to a reception theorist like Jauss, to seem fundamentally more interesting than ones that have just dawned upon the scene. Moreover, whereas some commentators have insisted upon the excitement of living through a profoundly innovative period, such as the late sixteenth century was for the English theatre, or the times of Pushkin and Lermontov for Russian prose, for someone like Jauss innovative activities such as these are best seen as something foregrounded against a background of previous activity. In other words, reception theory as practised hereabouts can cope with a process of gradual modification and change, but not with radical discontinuity and rupture.

This may not be too disabling a limitation, though, if gradual modification is a more typical state of affairs than radical discontinuity. It also means that some useful things can be said about the interrelationships of one text to another, or one form of discourse to another. For instance, at the beginning of this chapter I quoted a couple of passages by Jerome that made considerable use of a highflown style, with references to mermaids, Aeolian music, and so on. This can only make sense to a reader who has read (or who can at least imagine reading) passages of this kind that were intended to be taken straight, and Jerome is presumably banking on the reader responding negatively to the style in this instance in order to make a favourable response to the general raffishness which the Three Men so well exemplify. To this extent, then, we can enter the book in the catalogue of those that depend on parody of previous works or styles: *Tristram Shandy* has been the prime example used by everyone since the Russian formalist Shklovsky, but the phenomenon itself is far more ancient than this, and can be seen in such works as Euripides' savage and ironic treatment of the themes of previous Greek tragedians.

However, Jerome's text is in some ways more complex than this, and sequences such as that of the discovery of the drowned girl, written in essentially the same highflown style, are to all appearances offered 'straight' to the reader.

> She had wandered about the woods by the river's bank all day, and then, when evening fell and the grey twilight spread its dusky robe upon the waters, she stretched her arms out to the silent river that had known her sorrow and her joy.   (p. 160)

In cases such as this, the horizon of expectations has to be represented by a multiple rather than a single line, and what occurs is less a 'fusion of horizons' (a term Jauss borrowed from Gadamer) and more a shock to the reader who has to achieve a multiple and provisional interpretation of the text in question. In other words, it is not just a matter of taking an earlier world-view and adding our own onto it, a kind of civilized conveyence across time between tactful participants in a conversation, but rather a recognition that some gulfs cannot be bridged, that some conversations cannot be successfully managed.

Reception theory, as practised by Jauss, involves comparisons between actual, historically-located responses to text made by individuals or groups of individuals. Iser, in *The Act of Reading* (1976) is dealing with something that the sub-title of his book calls 'a theory of aesthetic response', and this appears to be something that is located within individual readers and also, despite that last word in the sub-title, within the text itself. What Iser is suggesting is that there are at least two components to literary text. One is the whole process of narrative flow, pretty much as was outlined in the second chapter of this book. The other is a process that feeds cues to the reader to which he has to make his own responses. In structuralist narratology there were indeed nuggets passed to the reader from time to time in the form of catalyzers, but the construct that was the narrative itself was securely located in an atemporal sphere, just like a mathematical formula. For Iser, though, reading is a process that takes place in real time, and this is important because the process of reading is one of discovery, even of self-discovery. Whereas for Jauss what disjunctures there were arose from the juxtaposition of different horizons of expectation—different historically-located images of what is and what is not possible—for Iser the text itself is intrinsically Delphic, creating blanks and indeterminacies that it is the reader's function to fill. The reader then proceeds dutifully to work his way, in real time, through the text, building up as he goes a more or less consistent picture of what the work is about. Suddenly, though, he can be challenged, brought face to face with a blank wall, made to wonder whether what he has taken to be a path through the novel is really perhaps a dead end. It is in these moments of truth that he makes discoveries, not only about the novel, but about himself as well, when he is forced to bring into consciousness, and into question, all his previously taken-for-granted assumptions.

Taken to an absurd extreme, such a position might seem to be like saying that the significant moments of cinema-going consist not of the images received ready-made by the retina, but of that proportion of the time when the screen is blank between frames of film, and the viewer has to construct an image for himself. This comparison would be misleading, though, in at least two ways. One is that the process undertaken in the cinema is by definition an unconscious one, whereas what Iser is describing are the moments of greatest self-awareness during the whole process of reading. The other is that the constructed image in the cinema is a passive repetition of what the eye has just seen, whereas Iser is thinking of a much more radical reorientation—as though the projectionist had suddenly shown by mistake a reel from a different film, and the viewer had to cope with the experience as best he could.

Just as was the case with Jauss, what we are considering here is an amalgam of textual structure and readerly experience, but with Iser the experience is located much more within the individual consciousness than within a collective one. 'Amalgam' may perhaps be the wrong word to choose, since Iser from time to time stresses that conflicting forces come into play, as when he speaks of

> the role offered by the text and the real reader's own disposition, and as the one can never be fully taken over by the other, there arises between the two the tension we have described. Generally, the role prescribed by the text will be the stronger, but the reader's own disposition will never disappear totally; it will tend instead to form the background to and a frame of reference for the act of grasping and comprehending.   (p. 37)

A corollary of this, of course, will be that different readings of the same text, by different individuals at the same time, or even by the same individual at different times in her life, will yield different results, since what the reader brings to bear on the text will be different. The range of possible readings will not, however, be infinite, since the structure of the text is the major determinant. Iser uses a familiar comparison with the work of a painter, who constructs the perspective of a painting in such a way that the real viewer is more or less obliged to adopt the viewpoint of the implied viewer. But there are differences as well. In a realist painting a simulacrum of a real view is provided, whereas text is a verbal construct without visual cues. The contents of a novel have therefore to be, in Iser's phrase, 'ideated'—that is, constructed mentally and non-visually—before they can be formed into meaning by the reader.

> But since this meaning is neither a given external reality nor a copy of the intended reader's own world, it is something that has to be ideated by the mind of the reader. A reality that has no existence of its own can only come into being by way of ideation, and so the structure of the text sets off a sequence of mental images which lead to the text translating itself into the reader's consciousness ... The concept of the implied reader offers a

> means of describing the process whereby textual structures are transmuted
> through ideational activities into personal experiences.   (p. 38)

The term 'relative autonomy', which has its origin in an altogether different part of the theoretical wood, can I think usefully be looked at here as a means of describing the process of ideation. Since each reader will carry out the process of ideation in different ways—ways that relate to her own individual thoughts and experiences—the term 'autonomy' can be justifiably employed. However, the structure of the text is in the last instance the determinant of the ideation, so that the autonomy is only relative.

Whereas for Jauss, then, the merely quirky and aberrant reading could be controlled or negated by the social norm of the horizon of expectations, for Iser the equivalent process is carried out by intratextual processes, and this control becomes all the more feasible since 'personal experiences' are, for Iser, just that—merely personal. Let us suppose that a group is studying Hopkins' poem 'The Wreck of the Deutschland'. If someone says 'We had a storm just like that on holiday last year', they are indeed calling on personal experience, but are not, in Iser's eyes, properly carrying out the process of ideation, since the textual determinants, involving concepts like suffering and redemption, are being wilfully or incompetently ignored.

It is worth noting just how comfortably Iser's model of the reading process accommodates itself to the liberal model of literary interpretation as it has been practised, in various guises, in educational institutions during this century. Great stress is laid on the pupil's experience (indeed in the more extreme versions this is described as the starting point) but the ultimate goal will be phrased as something like 'understanding what the poem has to say to us'. The process therefore moves from a multiplicity of starting points to a single, more or less predetermined, conclusion. Tales of storms encountered during holidays may therefore be acceptable as part of the warming-up process of discussion, but a point will be reached at which this recollected experience has to be transcended or subsumed into the dominant procedure of textual comprehension.

There is, too, another important way in which conversations about holidays, or even conversations about works of literature, differ from the essential act of reading as Iser sees it. Most conversations in general (though perhaps only a minority of those in classrooms) can be described as being symmetrical in nature, and each participant has the right to go back over what has been said by the other, to resolve ambiguities, and adopt various other strategies for arriving at a common and agreed conclusion. 'Conversations' with literary texts do not have this feature, since the literary text cannot be challenged or interrogated in a comparable way. Metalinguistic discourse can only be entered into with other readers, not with the text itself. This feature, which might be interpreted as a deficiency if we generalized outwards from a standard communicative

model, is a positive virtue for Iser. The blanks in the text, which cannot be
resolved by simple checking, cause the reader to pause and reassess his
own situation, thereby causing him to make educative discoveries about
the situation he finds himself in, or, even more valuably, about himself.

> Communication in literature, then, is a process set in motion and regulated
> not by a given code but by a mutually restrictive and magnifying interaction
> between the explicit and the implicit, between revelation and concealment.
> What is concealed spurs the reader into action, but this action is also
> controlled by what is revealed; the explicit in its turn is transformed when
> the implicit has been brought to light.   (pp. 168–9)

The curious and, in places, almost erotic vocabulary of this description
reminds me of several things. One is to be found in a collection of
marginalia written by William Blake. A Dr Thornton, in a commentary on
the Lord's Prayer, had written, 'Dim at best are the conceptions we have
of the Supreme Being, who, as it were, keeps the human race in suspense,
neither discovering, nor hiding himself'. By the side of this passage
Blake had written 'A female God!'. My point of comparison is that
Thornton's notions of the proper method of humble interrog-
ation of the Deity seem very like the way in which Iser envisages the
proper approach of the reader to the text. Iser's enterprise also seems
quasi-religious in intention, and Blake's deconstructive comment may be
equally apposite here too.

Another passage that Iser's description reminds me of, though, comes
in an essay by Barthes entitled 'Striptease' (1957). He writes (p. 84) that

> French striptease seems to stem from . . . a mystifying device which consists
> in inoculating the public with a touch of evil, the better to plunge it
> afterwards into a permanently immune Moral Good.

In Barthes' account, the accoutrements of the performance (gloves, fans,
etc.) introduce an element of exotic and threatening sexual evil which is
inseparable from their role of mystery and concealment. Once they are
removed, evil and threat are removed also, so that the spectators are left at
the end looking at 'nakedness as a natural vesture of woman, which
amounts in the end to regaining a perfectly chaste state of the flesh' (p. 85)

In much the same way, Iser's reader is required to experience a kind of
threat, an existential impasse, only in order to transcend the problem by
finally realigning himself with the text in all its purity. True reading, in
this view, is characterized by struggle and difficulty; if a reader effortlessly
projects the sum of his concepts onto the text and perceives nothing else
he is not engaging with the text at all. Yet if all the secrets of the text are
immediately apparent to the casual observer it can also be concluded that
the text itself lacks intrinsic merit.

From this struggle and engagement, though, quite extraordinary
benefits can accrue. Iser claims that

the reader can experience something previously not within his experience, and this something . . . ranges from a detached objectification of what he is entangled in, to an experience of himself that would otherwise be precluded by his entanglement in the pragmatic world around him. (p. 167)

It is virtually a commonplace of liberal theories that the experience of literature enables the diligent student to arrive at a greater degree of self-knowledge. But consider the vastness of Iser's claims here. Not only does the student come to experience her own self in a way that would otherwise be impossible, but she is also enabled to raise into consciousness the whole 'entanglement' of social and ideological forces that, by common consent, are inaccessible to humans for the rest of their waking and sleeping lives. Literature offers not just therapy and social analysis, but a unique form of cognition as well.

A claim of this kind seems sustainable only because Iser's theory of aesthetic response, like reception theory, combines attention to the message and to the addressee. Even so, many people will find it difficult to credit that this modified form of introspection can yield genuine knowledge of the kind that is attributed to it. That it can generate the conviction, on the part of the reader, that the experience amounts to the acquisition of knowledge, and that the knowledge is authentic, is of course easier to believe.

On the other hand, if we dismiss Iser's claims, what remains? In particular, for those who would wish to justify the place of literature teaching in the curriculum, what are the dangers of adopting a sceptical attitude towards this account of the reader's activities? Literature can, it is true, offer other forms of knowledge than those that have been outlined above, but it cannot so readily lay claims to uniqueness, and it may stand accused of relative inefficiency. For instance, it is possible to read *War and Peace* to get an account of Napoleon's Russian campaign, or even, it was once pointed out, to learn a recipe for strawberry jam, but the first item of information might be acquired with more, and more accurate, detail in any standard history, and the second would involve an act of reading that would last longer than the jamming season.

A more secure defence can perhaps be mounted by claiming that the process of ideation has a significant role to play in the development of a mature consciousness; that other varieties of text, because of their variously different functional roles, are significantly less capable of carrying out this task; that, in any event, other varieties of text within the curriculum are simply not encountered by the pupil to anything like the same quantitative extent, and would not be in most feasible alternative plans for the curriculum; and that, while literature is not and cannot be ideology-free any more than any other curriculum subject, it may offer significantly greater opportunities of analysing ideology. This last point, however, anticipates later discussions.

In all of the theoretical perspectives that have been examined above, it has been taken as axiomatic that, however great the degree of freedom of interpretation permitted to the reader, the text itself exercises a constraining force. Those black marks on the page do in the end provide a limit or boundary mark, beyond which the imagination cannot legitimately stray. In the more extreme versions of reader-oriented theory, however, this is not the case. In a collection of essays published under the title *Is There a Text in This Class?* (1980) Stanley Fish charts a process of movement away from the notion that those black marks have, in and of themselves, any authority whatsoever. I can best make the point by a comparison with those ambiguous drawings used by psychologists. One may be interpreted as either a rabbit or a duck; another can be taken to be either an old woman or a young girl. Once their ambiguous nature is realized, it is just not possible for the detached observer to assert any longer that that particular collection of lines is a depiction of a rabbit or of an old woman—merely that that is how some people see it, whereas another interpretation is possible. On the other hand, a group of students who have been pre-prompted by a discussion about ducks or about young girls will experience no difficulty whatsoever: they will see what they are by now expecting to see. For Fish, literary texts function in rather a similar way, except that interpretation is not limited to just two possibilities.

This begins to sound like the final collapse into anarchy of which due warning was issued earlier, but Fish is quick to reassure us. People won't in practice roam the streets insisting that *The Tale of Mrs Tittlemouse* is a novel about the Russian Revolution, and the reason he gives for allaying such fears is that no man is a readerly island; we all belong to what he terms interpretive communities. These consist of loose associations of people with tightly shared understandings of the realities of the worlds they inhabit. The convenience of seeing them as loose associations is that it relieves us of the troublesome business of defining the nature of the social grouping to which their members belong; we need not worry about social-class definitions, relationship to the means of production, or anything burdensome like that. On the other hand the shared understandings can represent remarkably powerful constraints.

We have most of us read newspaper accounts of extreme religious sects which are allegedly capable of persuading new recruits, in a remarkably short space of time, to accept a view of the world which is markedly different from that held by people in general. It is to Fish's credit that he has perceived that universities can function in a very similar way. In a by now famous passage he gives an account of events that occurred in a seminar room in which he was working. With his first group of the morning he wrote on the board the names of several distinguished linguists to whom he made reference; the question mark indicates he was unsure of the spelling of one of the names.

> Jacobs—Rosenbaum
>   Levin
>   Thorne
>   Hayes
>   Ohman (?)   (p. 323)

The next group to arrive had been studying English religious poetry of the
seventeenth century, in which the spatial arrangement of words on a page
is sometimes significant, and in which symbolic reference is often combined with didactic intent. Fish drew a frame around the names on the
board, and, informing the group that what they saw was a religious poem,
instructed them to interpret it. This they proceeded to do with a high
degree of intersubjective agreement; the following comment on the first
line of the 'poem' may be taken as typical of the rest of the discussion.

> Jacobs was explicated as a reference to Jacob's ladder, traditionally alle-
> gorized as a figure for the Christian ascent to heaven. In this poem,
> however ... the means of ascent is not a ladder but a tree, a rose tree or
> rosenbaum. This was seen to be an obvious reference to the Virgin Mary
> who was often characterized as a rose without thorns, itself an emblem of
> the immaculate conception.   (p. 324)

The feature of this analysis that Fish most wishes to call to our attention is
that all these meanings must of necessity have been projected onto the text
by the group, since what they were given is something that lacks syntactic
structure or semantic reference. The assertion he further makes is that
this act of reading is only an extreme case of a general process; something
like this is going on any time reading of any text takes place.

Let us admit straightaway that this discussion has many of the characteristics of the parlour game, and as such may be offensive to the serious-
minded. There are, however, other types of objection that can also be
made, and Fish has anticipated a good many of them. One is that the
names in question can in fact sustain semantic reference. The response to
this comes in two parts. The first, rather lamely, consists of an alternative
list of names, which just happens to have, in names such as Temple and
Church, precisely the same features which made the first list slightly
unusual. Fish's second point of defence, though, is more radical; he
claims that the process of interpretation would be the same

> even if there were no names on the list, if the paper or blackboard were
> blank; the blankness would present no problem to the interpreter, who
> would immediately see in it the void out of which God created the earth, or
> the abyss into which unregenerate sinners fall, or, in the best of all possible
> poems, both.   (p. 328)

The force of Fish's argument, then, is that it is the act of reading which is
itself constitutive. He has obliterated the conventional distinction between subjective and objective features, in which the text, the black marks
on the page, had certain irreducible objective features, and the individual

interpretation varied according to the personal, subjective characteristics of the reader. For Fish, objective data of this kind is inaccessible to human consciousness in any unmediated form, and individual interpretations cannot be merely personal because they arise of necessity within interpretive communities. Indeed, for Fish, problems would only begin to occur if groups failed consensually to arrive at interpretations of whatever they were presented with.

However, what Fish has failed to deal with in his account of the process is his own role as group leader with privileged access to power within the institution. He speaks of the work he sets the students as an 'assignment', but has no comment on the chain that leads from this through course grades to graduation, employment prospects, social mobility. In such a situation his capacity to define reality presumably exceeds that of the other members of the group, and a constrained consensus is hardly a surprising outcome. Moreover, the activity of studying religious poetry is not one that occurs in a vacuum either. We may guess that it is taking place within a society in which religious belief is permissible but not compulsory, and in which literature as an institution is valorized. These constitute social facts of a kind that extend further than the interpretive community in question, but have a considerable bearing upon its practices.

It is worth labouring these points a little because Fish's strategy, as he himself is the first to acknowledge, is one that challenges everything and changes nothing. He cheerfully states that his thesis

> is that whatever seems to you to be obvious and inescapable is only so within some institutional or conventional structure, and that means that you can never operate outside some such structure, even if you are persuaded by the thesis. (p. 370)

It is worth contrasting this with the way in which Iser's reader, who was not necessarily skilled in literary theory, was able, so to speak, to pull herself up by her own bootstraps, despite the fact that she was dealing with a much more 'objective' text than Fish would ever allow to exist. Fish may be right to point out that there is no necessary step from understanding the world to changing it, but that does not mean that there has to be an unbridgeable gulf either. By some forms of reckoning, at least, a recognition of the fact that interpretive communities are multiple and, in some senses, arbitrary in their forms of thought is a precondition for moving from one to another.

It is also worth bearing in mind that interpretive communities are not monolithic, all-encompassing institutions which control every aspect of their members' lives. One of Fish's students might have been a fundamentalist Christian, nursing a secret detestation for the Mariolatry he was being obliged to study in the text in question; another might have thought the exercise bunkum whilst being determined to shine in order to attract the attention of members of the opposite sex; a third might have enjoyed the exercise in the same way in which she liked solving crossword puzzles. Group dynamics would have heightened those characteristics which enabled task-oriented activity to take place, and suppressed those which would have led to discord, but there is no more reason to suppose this little interpretive community was a stable entity than there is to believe that Athenian slaves continued philosophical thought when released from a dialogue with Socrates.

Theories discussed in this chapter range from those in which the text creates the reader to those in which the reader creates the text. In whichever direction the process runs, though, it has been quite a solemn affair for the most part, characterized by a high ethical tone on the whole; even the jokiness of Fish's discussion is securely located within the bounds of the institution, much as seminarists may be permitted to make jokes about God. Yet to the laity the obvious omission from this whole discussion would surely seem to be any discussion of profane pleasure. After all, few people usually buy, borrow, or steal books in order to bring their construct system into line with that of an implied reader; more typically they do so in order to have a good time. Yet what constitutes a good time (and I have chosen this banal phrase in order to emphasize how shocking the whole idea is) is something that has received relatively little attention in academic studies. The only real exception to this statement is to be found amongst those working on topics relating to popular culture, and it is only in very recent years that their work has had a significant impact upon the larger academic community.

To say all this is not to ignore the fact that we have available to us a series of philosophical studies in aesthetics that extend across more than two millennia, or to ignore the work on this topic of some of the scholars already cited: Jauss and Barthes, for instance, have made distinguished contributions in this field. Rather it is to recognize the limitations of most ancient and many modern studies in respect of the particular issue referred to in the previous paragraph. If we discount all work that is prescriptive rather than descriptive, that immediately reduces the field considerably. If we required work to be securely grounded in empirical study, that would reduce it even more dramatically. And there is yet a further difficulty, because so much work in aesthetics has rested upon the distinction between subject and object, whilst some of the theorists we have looked at so far, and others that are still to come, consider this distinction invalid. Fish, for instance, would give the notion of pleasure derived from the detached contemplation of the autonomous work of art fairly short shrift. In such a perspective the only remaining pleasure comes from working on the text whilst recognizing its complete inaccessibility. I am somehow reminded of George Eliot translating Strauss's *Life of Jesus*, thrilling with horror at discovering its convincingly antireligious conclusions, and looking for support at a painting of Christ on her wall. Pleasure in such circumstances seems of a remarkably attenuated kind.

And still it moves. Pleasure in reading is a sufficiently widespread phenomenon that it can be found even in the school classroom or the university library. It is indeed something that can be attributed to the vagaries of interpretive communities, or to the effect of ideology upon the reader, but as an observable reality it obstinately persists and demands examination. Indeed, the point can be turned around, and the question asked the other way: if pleasure is not an outcome, how justifiable is the curriculum, and on what grounds? If that question is for the present left hanging in the air, at least that is a more satisfactory conclusion to a chapter devoted to reader response than one which contrives conveniently to suppress the question altogether.

4 Post-structuralism and the escape of signification

In the second chapter of this book, I pointed out that structuralism in its high and classical phase developed various narratological theories that purported to provide clear, scientific, and objective accounts of literary texts. In the third chapter, I described how some of the more radical relativists asserted that it was impossible to make any valid and objective statement whatsoever about any literary text. If I now assert that various aspects of post-structuralism have something in common with both these positions then clearly I shall have some explaining to do.

One obvious common element is the persons that were involved, as many of the early structuralists went on to develop very different positions from those with which they started—Barthes is a case in point. But another and more important consideration is that structuralism and post-structuralism, though they eventually became very different theoretical approaches, share certain common starting-points, of which perhaps the most important is the work of the founding father of modern linguistics, Ferdinand de Saussure (1857–1913).

A naïve view of language asserts that it consists of a series of names for things, rather as though we went around tying labels onto pre-existing objects. Saussure's use of the terms 'signifier' and 'signified' in contrast stresses that the set of sounds, or of marks on the page, (the signifier) and the concept thus named (the signified) are both equally arbitrary—they result from social convention rather than from any privileged access to the real world 'out there'. Signifier and signified are inseparable, like two sides of the same piece of paper, as Saussure put it. If we use the slightly different metaphor of two sides of a coin, this comparison can be developed in other directions as well. Like the coinage, the values represented by the process of signification cannot be defined as absolutes, but only in relation to the rest of the system to which they belong. Thus, in pre-decimal British currency, the only way to say what a shilling 'was' consisted of explaining that it was a twentieth of a pound, or that it was twelve pennies. And pounds and pennies in turn could only be defined by precisely the same means. This is what Saussure meant by talking of a system of differences without positive terms; it is impossible to say positively what threepence is when taken by itself, but it is possible to specify exactly how it relates to pence or pounds. No two coins are absolutely identical, after all, and there were times when silver threepenny bits and multi-sided alloy ones were simultaneously in circulation. The system of language, for Saussure, works in the same way; we cannot define a word such as 'mat' by pointing to a doormat, because that would not suffice as a definition of the kind of mat that is a place-mat on a dinner table. But what we can do is to say that, just as phonemically the signifier 'mat' is best defined as not being 'cat' or 'met' or 'map', so the signified concept 'mat' can best be defined contrastively in the same way.

At a phonemic level this works tolerably well; there are a limited number of phonemes in play in English, and a three-phoneme word such as 'mat' can therefore be defined as the product of a relatively small system. But against how many other signifieds does 'mat' have to be contrastively defined? One of the problems with the Saussurean system of language is that an individual has to know all of it before she can know any of it. To some extent this problem can be met by assuming that there is a series of synchronic systems, ranging from a child's first utterances to the fully developed adult language, and that the individual progresses dia-chronically from one to the next. At each stage language has to be a shared experience, since it is only through the ratification of others that the process of signifying can take place at all. With the final, adult version of the language the ratifying is carried out by other members of the wider speech community (a concept not too dissimilar to Fish's interpretive community), and here again a comparison with a monetary system may not be inappropriate. English banknotes are, objectively considered, only pieces of paper, and their validity as currency is attested by the signatures of officials of the Bank of England as representatives of the currency-using community.

This essentially social agreement on the system of a language Saussure terms 'langue' as opposed to speech ('parole') which is what we find in individual utterances. The business of signification only gets done through speech, but the validity of its transactions is derived from the ratification by language. This was why Barthes' *Introduction to the Structural Analysis of Narratives*, in *Image–Music–Text* (1966), took as its task the discovery of the 'langue' of narrative structure underlying the 'parole' of individual narratives. This, then, is the universally applicable, objective system that structuralism made it its business to discover.

Yet, as we all know in practice, meaning does not come as neatly packaged as that. If someone says 'The word "fanbelt" always makes me think of strawberries', that can perhaps be written off as a quirk or

aberration, though perhaps, to be systematic about it first, we ought to try
to discover whether there does not exist a sub-set of people within the
community for whom this association also holds good: perhaps a lot of
strawberries are bought from roadside stalls while people wait for their
car radiators to cool down. However, if I use the word 'fanbelt' a couple of
pages from now, there is some slight possibility that you will think of
strawberries as a result of reading this passage. You may even think of it if
you happen to come across the word in your car manual tomorrow. In this
fairly trivial example, then, we can see a very simple instance of the way in
which one text can leave traces on another. A good deal of literature offers
rather more interesting demonstrations of this process of intertextuality,
as it has been called. In Chapter Two, whilst discussing *The Adventures of
Tom Sawyer*, I briefly mentioned E. M. Forster's *A Passage to India* and its
crucial sequence set in the Marabar caves, and at that point I stressed the
differences between the two books. But consider the similarities as well.

Both books have a sequence in which a traumatic event in a cave
involves a male and female figure. The 'crime' that the female figure
commits involves the transgression of powerful social/sexual constraints—remember Becky was lying about where she was intending to
stay that night. In both cases the horror centres on a direct and powerful
experience of the utterly non-human nature of the physical universe.
Both events lead to the downfall of a non-white participant; in both the
restorative processes that society adopts involve the application of legal
sanctions and controls.

Now it would be possible to talk in traditional terms about the influence
of Twain upon Forster, and for all I know there may be a thesis
somewhere attesting precisely to this. But structuralism, like post-
structuralism, is grounded upon the death of the author, whose experiences and motives are not available to us for investigation—except, of
course, as texts themselves. And text was defined by the post-structuralist
Julia Kristeva as

> a translinguistic apparatus which redistributes the order of the language by
> putting a communicative utterance, aiming to inform directly, in relation
> with different utterances, anterior to or synchronic with it.   (1970, p. 12)

Various versions of reader-response theory would talk about the expectations and assumptions of people who had read Twain's novel before
they encountered Forster's. For teaching purposes it can often be extremely useful to map out readers' biographies in this way; consider how
useful a sequence it is to have read du Maurier's *Rebecca* before Brontë's
Jane Eyre, and both of them before James's *The Turn of the Screw*. But
notice that the sequence I have just offered is not a chronological one. It is
not 'influence' we are talking about here, but the generation of perceived
meaning. And for post-structuralism, as opposed to the other traditions I
have just mentioned, this surplus of unexpected, presumably unintended,

meaning over and above the proper and respectable proceedings involved in docoding narrative is a joyful scandal in which to revel.

For Saussurean linguistics, signifier and signified are totally separate categories even if, like love and marriage in the song, you can't have one without the other. For post-structuralism any number of misalliances are possible: each signified can act as signifier to another signified, and vice versa. What is more, there is no possible language of criticism, philosophy, or science which can somehow stand outside the fray; each forms part of a discourse which can be examined in its turn. There is no such thing as a metalanguage in which to talk about language, there is only language talking about language talking about language ...

How can we cope with a universe in which meaning is so multiple, so impermanent, so delusory? For Barthes in his post-structuralist phase, and for others as well, the best thing was to lie back and enjoy yourself. Perhaps not too supinely, though, because mere passive absorbtion of the single, overt meaning of the text is something he stigmatizes as mere consumption, whereas

> Full reading, on the contrary, is the kind in which the reader is nothing less than the one who desires to write, to give himself up to an erotic practice in language.   (Barthes, 1973a, p. 42)

This erotic practice, though, appears to be a solitary one, since the author, who as the originator of the utterance was, in Saussure's scheme of things, its ultimate validator, has been removed, assassinated, or dissolved into a play of competing textual features, and the text has been declared to be a non-material set of processes, unlike the book or the sound of the human voice which, in their material way, attest their single, irreducible presences.

A text is not a book; neither is it, in any simple and straightforward sense, a passage in a book either. Barthes reminds us of the etymological origin of the word—something woven out of separate strands. In much the same way every text is an intertext:

> Any text is a new tissue of past citations. Bits of code, formulae, rhythmic models, fragments of social languages, etc. pass into the text and are redistributed within it, for there is always language before and around the text.   (Barthes, 1973a, p. 39)

With such a complex artefact, varying readings are not only possible, they are positively obligatory. Again, this may sound a little like reader-response theory once more, but the differences are more important than the resemblances. There is no central core of meaning to be discovered, as there were in the more 'moderate' versions of that theory. There is no interpretive community available to validate wildly deviant readings, since the post-structuralist reader is to eschew mere 'consumption' of the text, and has instead to deconstruct it in his search for erotic pleasure. Finally, there is no stable self to be discovered by interaction with the text, since the self is as multiple and as written-through as the text is. In short, the whole humanist project of literary study has been comprehensively dismantled.

And yet, for Barthes, reading has a vital role to play in education—just as much, in its way, as it did for Leavis—though how differently. Criticizing the French educational system, he berates it for purporting to teach reading whilst giving no attention to the teaching of writing. His defence of the activity of reading-as-writing may therefore be seen as an attempt to swing the balance back the other way, to reinstate the practice of writing within the curriculum without reducing it to the sterility of the traditional teaching of rhetoric. If the pupils are not to be allowed to write creatively, then that creativity is to be invested in the reading process instead. Barthes' impulse here is a profoundly democratic one; he is maintaining that writing should not be limited to what he calls a caste of technicians— people such as writers, teachers, and intellectuals—but should instead be a universal experience. As against professional writers, he is extolling the amateur, whilst reminding us that the word can also indicate a lover.

The erotic experience of the text consists essentially of word-play, of turning the components of meaning around and about to yield senses that the author did not dream of, and perhaps could never have done. I said earlier that Barthes' impulse was a democratic one, and nowhere is this better shown than in his slogan 'the signifier belongs to everybody' (Barthes, 1973a, p. 37). The challenge to the proprietorial rights of the author over the text is plain for all to see. However, applying Barthes' own principle that 'the intertext is a general field ... of unconscious or automatic quotations, given without quotation marks' (ibid, p. 39), I in turn can suggest that what we have here is a version of Proudhon's 'property is theft', and apply to Barthes also the criticism that Marx made of Proudhon that he obviously remained trapped within the paradigm of bourgeois property-owning.

The other curiosity of Barthes' position is that, having set about deconstructing the text, he then proceeds to reify it again—indeed virtually to anthropomorphize it. In the previous paragraph I quoted only one half of a sentence; the complete version runs 'the signifier belongs to everybody; it is the text which, in fact, works tirelessly, not the artist or the consumer'. We should, of course, remember that 'consumer' means not the valorized and inventive reader but the inert and unimaginative one. Even so, it is in a way remarkable that this capacity for action should be attributed to a non-material text, and perhaps it indicates how much residual idealism there still was in Barthes' philosophical stance.

In Chapter Two, discussing Barthes' theory of the functioning of narrative, I quoted him as saying that 'another semiotic' was needed to complete the connection between the structure of the text and the structure of the society in which it is located. By the time Barthes had finished his self-transformation into a post-structuralist, he saw this connection as being achieved not by a semiotic but by the play of codes through the text.

He provides his classic definition of what these codes are in *S/Z* (1970), a study of a short story by Balzac. It is illuminating to compare not only the theory but also the method of this book with that of the essay discussed in Chapter Two. As opposed to the precisely defined narrative units of that earlier work, Barthes now deals in units termed 'lexias', which are quite arbitrary, provisional and somewhat akin to the outcome of a particular reading strategy at a particular time. Moreover, each lexia can manifest the functioning of one or several of the codes he is discussing; there is no exact matching of structure and function involved.

Though *S/Z* deals with five codes, there is nothing final or absolute about this figure either; indeed in an essay written three years later (Barthes, 1973b) he adds another to his scheme, and indicates that any number of others can be included in the list in due course. The original five, however, can be described in the following way.

The first, the hermeneutic code, consists of the setting up of riddles or mysteries within the text which are to be solved or revealed later. This is obviously highly reminiscent of the functioning of nuclei as discussed in the earlier work. The second code, the semic, deals with the manipulation of information about characters or places or things. To a degree, once more, this can be related back to the way that informants worked in the earlier scheme. The third code, the symbolic, provides information that is grist to the mill of the classificatory processes of the human psyche—such things as implied or stated antitheses, for instance. The fourth code, the proairetic, has to do with actions and is, like the first one, concerned with narrative flow, but whereas the hermeneutic code deals with enigmas that cannot be resolved at that stage of the game, the proairetic is concerned with actions for which a typical outcome can be confidently predicted. The fifth code, the cultural one, is a representation of the collective stock-in-trade of human society, its habitual and taken-for-granted beliefs, habits and assumptions.

Put briefly like this, Barthes' system of codes is likely to elicit nothing more than amazed incomprehension on first acquaintance, and one suspects that Barthes would not have been too displeased with this first reaction. However, he is also concerned to be a teacher, even if a Delphic one, and he points out that the title and first sentence of the story he is examining provide examples of all five of his codes:

Sarrasine
I was deep in one of those daydreams which overtake even the shallowest of men, in the midst of the most tumultuous parties.   (pp. 17–18)

Here the title illustrates the hermeneutic code; we recognize it as the name of a person, but have yet to discover who and what that person is. The 'e' ending to the name indicates, in French, that the person or object referred to is of the feminine gender, and is an instance of the semic code. The development of the story is to hinge on a series of contrasts: hot/cold, inside/outside, and so on. Barthes claims that the reference to 'daydreams' therefore cues in this whole symbolic code; frankly, I think he cheats a little here in order to discover all five codes in the first sentence. However, we recognize that a daydream in narrative is, like a piecrust, made to be broken, and this recognition is an instance of the proairetic code. Finally, parties. It is assumed by the story that we all know what parties can be like, and this pre-existing knowledge waiting to be tapped constitutes the cultural code.

It can be seen that this list is neither categorical nor exclusive. I challenged its application in one instance, and Barthes would have hardly been in a position to disagree, since he is the first to insist that a text is a terrain traversed by codes rather than one that is dotted with them like boulders. And indeed three years later, as I indicated above, he added in a further code, the code of communication or exchange, which deals with the signs of people addressing each other. Indeed it is essential to his way of seeing things in the early 1970s that any system of description should not pretend to be total and absolute, but should admit of further change and development. Barthes was a natural system-builder with a strong urge to destroy or subvert systems.

Let us return briefly to the Saussurean definition of signifier and signified. On the one hand, the system only operated at all because of the web of contrasts with all the other signifiers and all the other signifieds. In this sense it is therefore quite correct to say that Saussure was primarily interested in 'langue' rather than 'parole', that is to say in language rather than speech. On the other hand, the 'langue' of any given language is inaccessible in its entirety, and can only be approached indirectly through examples drawn from 'parole'. In this sense at least 'parole' can be held to validate 'langue'. This assumption that direct person-to-person experience provides some sort of guarantee of authenticity is deeply embedded in the European tradition of thought; perhaps so deeply that we are not always aware of its existence. Examples can be found at most times from that of Socrates to the present, but, as this book is concerned with English teaching, perhaps a literary example will be most appropriate.

In *Othello*, the Moor is persuaded by Iago that his wife Desdemona is unfaithful to him. The 'proofs' that Iago offers are items of indirect, circumstantial evidence, and are, as the audience recognizes, misleading. They amount, in effect, to texts, and the most celebrated one, the handkerchief, is a text in the etymological sense quoted above as well; it is a veritable tissue of lies. Indeed, recounting the alleged magic properties of the handkerchief, Othello greatly enhances its status as a signifier. What Iago and Othello jointly undertake is a reading of the text, with Othello, the outsider in Venetian society, at a disadvantage when it comes to coping with the cultural code. Othello is, however, enough of a European to demand ocular proof and, failing that, verbal evidence. Planting Othello where he can see but not hear properly, Iago engages Cassio, the alleged lover, in conversation about his whore Bianca. Cassio's all-too-expressive gestures confirm Othello in his suspicions. In other words, Othello fails here to deploy effectively the code of communication or exchange; the reference to persons in Cassio's responses is misapprehended.

The fourth Act of the play provides further material for those who wish to see Othello's downfall as that of an incompetent reader. One of his comments hurled at Desdemona is

> Was this fair paper, this most goodly book
> Made to write 'whore' upon?   (Scene 2, lines 71–2)

The material evidence, Desdemona's person, is seen as incapable of communication, whereas, in his logocentric obsession, Othello is aware only of the process of signification centring on the concept of 'whore'.

Desdemona, however, has linguistic problems of her own. She says (lines 161–2):

> I cannot say 'whore'.
> It does abhor me now I speak the word.

In making the metalinguistic comment about what she is unable to say, Desdemona says it, thereby not only providing a logical contradiction and a transgression of a taboo at one and the same time, but also reminding us that metalinguistic comment is linguistic utterance and as susceptible to analysis as anything else. Perhaps the best comments to offer on this curious utterance, though, are those of Barthes when writing (1973b) of a short story by Edgar Allan Poe in which a dying man is placed under hypnosis and, when dead, produces the utterance 'I am dead!'. Barthes comments, 'What is said is no other than this impossibility: the sentence is not descriptive, it is not constative, it delivers no message other than its own enunciation' (p. 153). Later (p. 154) he adds 'the unheard-of sentence ... is in no way the unbelievable utterance, but much more radically the impossible enunciation'. The relationship of signifier and signified is here irretrievably shattered.

The fifth Act of the play yields one more example relevant to our present concerns. In the deathbed scene Othello finally accuses Desdemona directly of having given the handkerchief to Cassio. Desdemona, true to the last to the phonocentric tradition, replies simply 'Send for the man and ask him' (Scene 2, line 50). Othello's response ignores this suggestion and concentrates instead on the enunciation he has just heard: 'Take heed of perjury, thou art on thy deathbed' (line 51). Doomed to remain an incompetent analyst of texts in a society fixated on the self-validating immediacy of conversation, if is only when it is too late that he gestures towards this belief himself:

> CASSIO: Dear general, I never gave you cause.
> OTHELLO: I do believe it, and I ask your pardon.
>   (Scene 2, lines 299–300)

By now, however, he is trapped within his own oxymoron, 'an honourable murderer' as he terms himself, and his eventual move towards suicide is prefaced with an account of how he has, on the one hand, killed a noble Venetian lady but, on the other, how he once slew a Turk for traducing that state; his appeal for justification centres on a use of the symbolic code. 'Set you down this' (line 351) is his cry, so that to the last his misplaced confidence lies in what he foolishly considers the univocal medium of text.

This analysis is of course perverse, though, I hope, illuminating as well. If it seems shocking, this may be because, in the naturalist tradition, we are accustomed to thinking of characters in novels or plays as being akin to real people, so that to speak of them as texts seems to be an action that robs them somehow of human dignity. Barthes' enterprise, throughout the varying stances he adopted in his life, consisted of an assault upon this belief and an insistence that the writerly text, in which the reader actively produced meaning, was infinitely to be preferred to the readerly text, in which the consumer was restricted to reproducing the intended meaning enshrined in the text by the godlike author.

Many of these strategies and insights were adopted by Jacques Derrida, the highly influential French post-structuralist, whose work has proved seminal both in European philosophy and literary theory, and in the development of deconstruction as currently practised in the United States of America. But it is easier to be influenced by him than to paraphrase him, as many commentators have found to their cost. Three major volumes of his work appeared virtually simultaneously in French in 1967, and in English translation at various times during the 1970s. Their style is tantalizing, allusive, and stimulating rather than directly informative, and they do not lend themselves readily to brief quotation. It is for this reason that I have spent some time in this chapter in preparing the ground for a discussion of some of his principal themes.

The most useful place to start is perhaps with his concept of text, where his position is extremely similar to that of Barthes. Here his slogan is that there is nothing outside the text, which we can paraphrase as meaning that there is not anything which is not textual in nature. In contrast the phonocentric, logocentric tradition to which I referred earlier esteems all language only in order to pass through it, to transcend it in order to reach an ultimate ground of being—absolute truth, God, whatever. Speech in this tradition is more authentic than writing, because it stands nearer to the source of utterance, is validated by the attestation of the utterer and is more likely to lead to a knowledge of truth than is a written text, which can be exposed to all manner of sophistries. And historically speech is deemed to precede writing in human use, so that somewhere in the argument there lurks the assumption that a form that is primordial is more authentic, more revelatory of human and metaphysical essence.

Derrida stands this argument on its head and asserts that writing is not a particular use of speech, but that speech is one manifestation of writing. This is not intended to conjure up an image of cavemen with fountain pens; rather, to assert that speech does not bubble up from some un-polluted well but is as much a social artefact as anything that tumbles off the rotary presses. It is therefore fitting that, in *Of Grammatology* (1967a), he should have written at some length of Rousseau, since the concept of 'natural' man as good and 'social' man as degenerate finds a classic expression in the latter's work. Derrida does not so much challenge Rousseau directly as point out the contradictions and presumably unin-tended meanings in Rousseau's writings; in other words, he emphasizes their textuality. For instance, Rousseau extols moments from his past life as points of pure and blissful perception. To do so, however, he has of necessity to have recourse to language, since this is the only way open to him to retrieve the past. This language is not the pure, authentic cry of the noble savage in which, Rousseau said, humanity 'first gave every single word the sense of a whole proposition', but the language we know, the language of syntax, of common nouns, a language which, by generalizing, distances and postpones the recapturing of the experience that is being signified. The way that Derrida puts this is to say that 'Language *adds itself* to presence and supplants it, defers it within the indestructible desire to rejoin it' (p. 280).

This notion of deferral is one of Derrida's key terms, and forms one element of a complex word-play in which he indulges in order to elaborate his meaning. On the one hand, it is possible to say that language defers to presence as the supreme authenticity, and yet on the other hand, by deferring *ad infinitum* the experience of that authenticity, it differs from it, bearing away on a track of its own which will never rejoin the original. As a portmanteau word to indicate both deferral and difference, Derrida using a neologism speaks of (though we should now say writes) 'différance'—and, etymologically responding, we can well credit that it bears cloaks: polymorphous shape without form or content, the supreme signifier without a signified.

Discussing writing as a notation of speech, Rousseau pointed out that what it lacks is any indication of the inflections of the voice which make speech specific to one time, place, and situation. It would in principle be possible to supplement writing with a commentary which gave some indications along these lines, but this would rapidly prove tedious to all concerned. Rousseau terms such a commentary a supplement and Derrida plays upon this term and its alternative meaning of supplanting something.

> If supplementarity is a necessarily indefinite process, writing is the supple-ment *par excellence* since it marks the point where the supplement proposes itself as supplement of supplement, sign of sign, *taking the place of* a speech already significant: it displaces the *proper place* of the sentence, the unique time of the sentence pronounced *hic et nunc* by an irreplaceable subject, and in return enervates the voice. It marks the place of the original doubling.
>
> (p. 281)

If Rousseau saw this original face-to-face communication as akin to the Garden of Eden, then Derrida rejoices in the Fall, a *felix culpa* or happy catastrophe which, in taking humanity out of the presence of the Great Signifier, plants us instead firmly in a world in which texts are a more than sufficient substitute; texts that are seen not as The Word, leading unequivocally back once more to presence, but as words upon words that redouble and multiply meanings as they are read. The supplement, after all, is something over and above, something extra, the pastry that is embarrassingly and provokingly left over when all the shells have been neatly cut out and matched with their portion of jam.

I have recourse to metaphors, but is is well known that the dyer's hand takes the colour of what it is steeped in. I am also attempting to provide an introduction to a passage from *Writing and Difference* (1967b). Here Derrida first quotes the fourth-century Bishop of Constantinople, St John Chrysostom, who prescribed openness to the Spirit as the best course for humanity, so that our hearts might be written on as books are with ink. Failing that, though, the personal study of the Scriptures was recommended as the second-best course. It can be seen that the appellation 'Chrysostom' ('golden-mouth') is appropriately phonocentric in its emphasis. Derrida comments:

> But, all faith or theological assurance aside, is not the experience of *secondarity* tied to the strange redoubling by means of which constituted—written—meaning presents itself as prerequisitely and simultaneously *read*: and does not meaning present itself as such at the point at which the other is found, the other who maintains both the vigil and the back-and-forth motion, the work, that comes between writing and reading, making this work irreducible? Meaning is neither before nor after the act. Is not that which is called God, that which imprints every human course and recourse with its secondarity, the passageway of deferred reciprocity between reading and writing? (p. 11)

More matter, with less art! Perhaps, yet, though 'tis madness, yet there's method in it. Madness was indeed one form of discourse which preoccupied one of Derrida's contemporaries, Michel Foucault, not necessarily so much for what it said as because it was typically inaccessible to the investigator/reader, being so effectively policed by the guardians of what was to be deemed normal and what was not that the words of the 'mad' were censored so as not to come to the hearing of the sane. The only real exception to this process was to be found in literature, itself a privileged form of deviant discourse.

Foucault undertook detailed examinations of the workings of social institutions such as the law or medicine, and their realization in physical institutions such as prisons or hospitals. The social institution of education, and its realization in schooling, would be in many ways a natural addition to this list, but in fact was not one that received such extensive treatment from him. To say that he was interested in the history of institutions, then, is true up to a point, but such a formulation reduces the scope of his achievement, which included also a reassessment of what the practice of history itself consisted of.

In his introduction to *The Archaeology of Knowledge* (1969), a book written after his more detailed treatment of some of the institutions listed above, Foucault outlines his approach to the more general question of what it is to write history. The historian has always been faced with the problem of how to define units of analysis, and on what scale to set about the interpretation of events. Any narrative approach that deals purely in linear processes of causality is failing to deal with the breaks and discontinuities of historical processes. Any attempt to write a 'total history' is falling into a sub-Hegelian trap of assuming that all features of a period can be reduced to, or derived from, a single, transcendental essence.

In turning away from the notion of access to a truth that lay behind appearances, Foucault was turning away from Hegel and turning towards Nietzsche. This can be seen in his comments on how scholars have treated the documents they have examined. They have traditionally looked at whether these aimed to be truthful or misleading, and whether their texts were authentic or corrupt. Implicit in this approach was the assumption that the document was 'the language of a voice since reduced to silence, its fragile, but possibly decipherable trace' (1969, p. 6) In contrast to this, the approach to the practice of history now

> organizes the document, divides it up, distributes it, orders it, arranges it in levels, establishes series, distinguishes between what is relevant and what is not, discovers elements, refines unities, describes relations. (pp. 6–7)

Such a project can be seen to have much in common with the structuralist approach to the study of literary texts, where also the notion of direct access to truths conveyed by literature had been replaced by a commitment to analyse, order, classify, and serialize.

But Foucault goes beyond stucturalism in his comments on historical method. The element of discontinuity is for him a crucial one: discontinuity in the subject matter of the historian, so that breaks and points of rupture in the continuity of a series can be identified, and discontinuity also in the historian's own method, so that the writer of history can become distanced from the process that is the object of analysis.

All this may seem some way from the analysis of literary texts, but Foucault explicitly compares the two processes in his comment on

> literary analysis, which now takes as its unity, not the spirit or sensibility of a period, nor 'groups', 'schools', 'generations', or 'movements', nor even the personality of the author, in the interplay of his life and his 'creation', but the particular structure of a given *oeuvre*, book, or text.   (p. 5)

It is also useful to compare Foucault's comments on the constitution of the object of investigation in historical study with the analogous process in the analysis of literary texts. Three paragraphs back, I drew a parallel between the approach to historical and literary texts within a structuralist mode, but it is helpful also to compare Foucault's emphasis on breaks that are themselves the product of the practice of analysis, with Barthes' views, as expressed in *S/Z*, on the definition of lexias, which are themselves constituted by the act of reading, even whilst they provide evidence, in their almost arbitrary isolation from the rest of the text, of the action of codes within the text as a whole.

Foucault's position is basically an anti-humanist one, challenging the notion that individual human beings are central, either in value or in fact, to the processes of history. Instead he sees humans as constituted by history, not as integral and separate beings, but in something like the way in which texts are, and characterized like them by breaks and discontinuities internal to that allegedly whole and seamless unit, the human personality.

Structuralism, itself for the most part an anti-humanist set of assumptions and practices, took the science of linguistics as its model for the procedures and modes of analysis of the other human sciences. Barthes indeed wished at one stage to incorporate the other sciences under the overarching structure of an expanded linguistics. Foucault in his later years was keen to deny that he had ever been a structuralist, but what he did concede was that he had unduly emphasized the role of discourse as a linguistic rather than a social practice and, in so doing, had played down those social relationships, such as those involved in the exercise of power, that had an origin in some other realm of social activity than the purely semiotic.

Quite what was the origin of power in Foucault's scheme of things was something quite difficult to establish. That it constituted and defined individuals, however, was clear enough. In a celebrated discussion (1979) of Bentham's *Panopticon* (1791) Foucault illustrates how he saw the process. The 'Panopticon' was a general model for all total institutions in which the subjects were ranged in cells at the circumference of a circle, deprived of the ability to communicate one with another, but perpetually subject to observation from the windows of a central tower. Behaviour modification could then be undertaken, and the results monitored. The subjects knew that they were subject to observation, but did not know when they were being observed. They therefore became the first, best monitors of their own actions. The knowledge thus generated, both within the observer and within the observed, was an outcome of the exercise of power, but separable from that power.

Bentham's design is usually thought of as prepared for a prison, but is in principle suitable to various institutions; substitute aural for visual monitoring, and it becomes a passable description of a language laboratory, for example. It is also worth noting that the organization of space constitutes the observed as much as the observers, prescribing actions and relationships—a phenomenon that may be recognizable to even more teachers than those of foreign languages. Foucault comments elsewhere

> In this form of management, power is not totally entrusted to someone who would exercise it alone, over others, in an absolute fashion; rather this machine is one in which everyone is caught, those who exercise this power as well as those who are subjected to it. (1977, p. 156)

Comments such as these may help to explain what Foucault means when he says:

> Maybe the target nowadays is not to discover what we are, but to refuse what we are. We have to imagine and to build up what we could be to get rid of this kind of political 'double bind', which is the simultaneous individualization and totalization of modern power structures. (1982, p. 216)

These last two terms warrant some further comment. We tend to think of the modern state as dealing with people in whole groups or classes at a time, rather than as separate individuals. It is part of Foucault's argument, however, that it is state power which constitutes individuals as individuals in the first place, and that this is done through a whole series of intermediary institutions, such as 'the family, medicine, psychiatry, education, and employers' (p. 215).

Later in the same essay he writes:

> Take for example an educational institution: the disposal of its space, the meticulous regulations which govern its internal life, the different activities which are organized there ... The activity which ensures apprenticeship and the acquisition of aptitudes or types of behaviour is developed there by means of a whole ensemble of regulated communications (lessons, questions and answers, orders, exhortations, coded signs of obedience, differentiation marks of the 'value' of each person and of the levels of knowledge) and by the means of a whole series of power processes (enclosure, surveillance, reward and punishment, the pyramidal hierarchy.) (pp. 218–9)

It should be noted here that Foucault distinguishes between relationships of communication, such as when a teacher asks a question and a pupil answers it, and relationships of power, such as when a teacher establishes that she has the right to determine the agenda of a lesson. Any communicative activity is in some sense a way of acting upon someone else, but, for Foucault, the exercise of power is something stronger than this, since power relations have a specific nature, even if they are achieved through the medium of communicative systems. Thus, though semiotic analysis can be applied to the communications which constitute the 'text' of the lesson, its explanatory effectiveness in relation to the totality of the situation is strictly limited. It is of course in staking out a position such as this that Foucault is most overtly seeking to distance himself from that stance of neutrally scientific and linguistically-based objectivity adopted by the earlier phase of structuralism.

These two spheres—the relationships of communication and the relationships of power—are for Foucault two categories for the analysis of human activity. The third one that is to be added to this list is productive work, or, as he terms it, the 'transformation of the real' (p. 218). Since one function of a school is the transmission of work skills, this was what Foucault was referring to, in the passage quoted two paragraphs back, as 'apprenticeship and the acquisition of aptitudes'. In, let us say, a technology lesson, this tripartite analysis is easy to apply: pupils acquire skills in the manipulation of physical matter; a communicative code ensures, through the use of spoken language, or perhaps through worksheets, that the transmission of skills can be effected; and, finally, habits of obedience, docility and deference are inculcated. Where it is less easy to apply this analysis, though, is in a literature lesson, where the 'manipulative skills' involved consist of nothing other than the study of the use of the communicative code itself, which thereby is perpetually in imminent danger of becoming the clearly apparent subject matter of the lesson rather than the transparent medium through which it operates.

This 'peril' to which I am drawing attention here is very much in accordance with the view that Foucault takes of the situation. Though for him Power is all-pervasive it cannot be total. Complete control on the one hand and complete subjection on the other would simply produce passive inertia, whereas for him the essence of power relationships is that they are characterized by struggle and by nodes of resistance. By the same token, Power does not exist as an abstraction (despite that capital letter) since it only exists in and through activity.

> It is ... always a way of acting upon an acting subject or acting subjects by virtue of their acting or being capable of action. A set of actions upon other actions.   (p. 220)

So we are faced with something akin to a paradox here. On the one hand the process of schooling in general, and that of literature teaching in particular, is characterized by the rational and economic deployment of resources within institutions, which Foucault sees as characteristic of European societies since the eighteenth century, and of which the Panopticon can serve as both emblem and example. On the other, that very concentration of people and of resources within the institution and, as I suggested above, the tightrope nature of the subject matter, can also generate forms of resistance which symbiotically make that exercise of power what it is. This 'agonism', as Foucault terms it, deriving his expression from the Greek term for struggle, can be seen henceforward as the characteristic activity of the classroom reader; and if the process sounds on the whole less agreeable than Barthes' erotic imagery it may, by the same token, by more in accord with common experience.

Just as the literature *on* madness did not characteristically permit the mad to speak—to produce a literature *of* madness (unless of course it was Literature)—so the literature *on* schooling has not characteristically had much truck with a literature *of* schooling, which might be a record of pupils' own responses to institutional experience. There are, of course,

exceptions to both these assertions, but many of the exceptions themselves also betray a certain symmetry. In psychiatry the utterances of the
mad play a diagnostic role (a further instance of disruption of the relationship between signifier and signified). Similarly, in English lessons the
label 'creative writing' is frequently a euphemism for the monitoring and
correction of orthographic skills. Self-monitoring has also an important
role to play in the development of orthographic skills, just as prisoners in
the Panopticon were brought into a position in which they were compelled
to be their own first, best gaolers, or patients in psychotherapy are
required to verbalize their condition in order to effect a cure.

There are of course other and more positive instances of a literature of
schooling than these, though. The development, during the last twenty
years or so, of an interest in classroom discourse within a tradition of
linguistics is a case in point. Another example would be the studies of the
role of co-operative dialogue in the development of pupils' concept
formation. However, valuable though these inquiries may seem to be,
they are themselves subject to one of Foucault's double-binds, since,
being undertaken (of necessity) from within the perspective of the edu-
cator, they can hardly claim to be the unmediated perceptions of the
pupils themselves. So in the end we are again reduced to the single
privileged case that Foucault allows to have occurred, which in this
instance would be the records, in autobiographies or in works of fiction, of
the experiences of schooling, and specifically of the study of literature, as
recounted by the pupils themselves.

Even here, though, post-structuralism will not, so to speak, leave us to
our reading in peace, but reminds us that the text we study does not
re-create the original living voice, let alone the experience to which it
might wish to testify, but is as full of lacunae, of contradictions, and of
competing codes and discourses as a courtroom in which a trial cannot
either properly begin or properly end.

5   Macherey and the triple dialectic

In the work of Foucault, we saw power discussed as something all-pervasive throughout human society. Similarly, resistance to that power, though not equally distributed through human individuals or groups, was in many ways a universal characteristic. In this and in other respects it is interesting to compare him with the French philosopher and literary theorist Pierre Macherey, whose work is quite explicitly located within the tradition and practices of French Marxism and, more specifically, that part of it which is directly influenced by the writings of Louis Althusser.

It is impossible to summarize in a couple of paragraphs the various debates and disputes which eventually produced the key definitions in this area. A few co-ordinates must however be provided if the ground is to be covered at all. As is well known, Marx adopted the principle of the dialectic of history from Hegel, but claimed that in doing so he had rejected the mystical and idealist shell of Hegel's thought whilst retaining the rational kernel, which consisted of the dialectic itself; hence dialectical materialism. In its application to later political and literary-theoretical debates, in particular over the vexed question of 'socialist realism' during the Stalinist era, dialectical materialism was therefore held to assign absolute primacy to the economic and social base in any given society, and to relegate beliefs, customs, and cultural products of any kind to the realm of the superstructure, where they led a directly determined, and generally secondary, kind of existence. All that literature was therefore able to do was to reflect the relations at the base of the society that generated it, and the best literature was that which best reflected those relations.

In opposition to such a reductionist stance, Macherey has established various positions, one of which, in a recent essay, he describes as an attempt to philosophize 'in a materialist way' (1983, p. 136). The slight tentativeness of this phrase is deliberate, since he contrasts the approach with 'Dialectical Materialism' (the capitalization and diacritics are Macherey's own) which he sees as a monolithic and fundamentally unsatisfactory enterprise attempting to generate universal laws concerning the behaviour of matter. For Macherey this may be 'Materialism', but it is certainly not dialectical.

His own brand of philosophy, by contrast, is one which is an intervention within the field of philosophical discourses, rather than one which by a promulgation of laws creates and defines its own proper object of study. By adopting this much more modest-seeming position, Macherey is also recognizing that philosophical discourse, like other discourses, is situated within history and subject to historical forces, rather than commenting, god-like, from a position somewhere above the fray. This recognition of situatedness, though, is a strength rather than a weakness. A pseudo-science, which creates and demarcates as a field of study the behaviour of objects in the real world, can in the end only abase itself before the plenitude of their existence, submitting its own reality entirely to the richness of that which it comments on. In that respect, I might interpolate here, it can be held to resemble that kind of descriptive literary criticism which defines a literary text as an object of study only in order to submit to it the more completely—the kind of approach which Macherey in an earlier work, *A Theory of Literary Production* (1966) labelled 'criticism as appreciation (the education of taste)' (p. 3).

In defining his own work as an intervention and as one discourse amongst many, Macherey might seem to be adopting a position of total relativity rather akin to that of Derrida described earlier. However, this is something that he would want to distance himself from in various ways. In his earlier work he contrasted 'criticism as appreciation' with 'criticism as knowledge', which he characterizes as the 'science of literary production' (p. 4). It is tempting to translate these terms back into others with which we are more familiar, and to equate them with other paired terms such as arts and sciences, or imagination and reality. Such an approach would however be a mistake, even though it recognizes that Macherey valorizes the second of these two terms.

Macherey argues that criticism as appreciation is inescapably a product of the superstructure, is inescapably restricted to that sphere, and is one means amongst many by which the dominant ideology is reproduced from generation to generation. If inter-class relations are to persist through a period of time greater than one lifespan, newcomers to the system must be taught positions to take up within it, and they are taught this most effectively when they believe that there is no alternative. Following Althusser, whose key work on this subject appeared in 1970, Macherey later went on to distinguish between two means by which this result can be achieved. One, the more blatant and overt, consists of the Repressive State Apparatus or RSA. This consists of the actual or potential use of the physical force at the command of the State. An example of this, drawn from the 1980s, would be the use of troops and police to compel black pupils into school attendance during a boycott in South Africa. The alternative and more covert means consists of the Ideological State Apparatus or ISA. This comprises a set of institutions which varies from society to society and from time to time; a representative list for our culture, however, would include churches, trade unions, the family and the educational system. Indeed, Althusser asserts that education is the most powerful ISA in contemporary society, having assumed the role previously played by the churches. Thus, whereas a RSA would compel pupils to attend school, an ISA would teach them attitudes of subservience and docility once they got there. For Althusser, it is important to note, an ISA can therefore, so to speak, undertake crucial initiatives of its own; it is much more than a pale reflection of certain underlying economic realities.

For those reared within a tradition of liberal humanism, statements such as that last one offer an opportunity, it would seem, to adopt the more acceptable bits and pieces of Althusser's thinking and to incorporate them into an only slightly expanded liberal model of social processes. If initiatives can be undertaken within spheres such as the educational one, the argument runs, and if these initiatives are relatively autonomous in respect of other aspects of economic and social change, then this only confirms what we have been saying all along: literature can change people's lives, and it occupies a space which is separate from daily life, but from which daily life can be commented on. It is therefore an intellectual marketplace in which views can be exchanged—and may the best view win.

Neither Althusser or Macherey would have any truck with this. First, the autonomy that is ascribed to the ISA is only relative, so that the base remains in the model as the ultimate determinant. Secondly, the notion of autonomous individuals making free and unconstrained choices assumes that those individuals existed as individuals before the moment of choice, whereas in Althusser's scheme of things the role of the individual is actually created by the ISA itself. If a man whistles and finds that a puppy is following him, then the roles of master and mastered have been created by that act of whistling. Althusser term the process 'interpellation', and provides an example of his own that I shall consider later. In the same way, for Althusser, the prime function of Western literature is to create in the reader the delusion that she is a free and unconstrained individual, one who actually chose the process that (in reality) was what constituted her.

The one thing that offers a means of escape from this perpetual cycle of the reproduction of ideology is the practice of criticism as knowledge. By this means the critic can determine what ideological forces are in play within the text that is being studied. The approach of 'Dialectical Materialism' was to allege that there was just one discourse to be found in the text—that which was directly determined by the base relations of the society in question. Macherey, in contrast, sees the text as traversed by various ideologies, and it is this recognition of the internally contradictory nature of any given text which makes him at times resemble other post-structuralists in their forms of analysis. Where they would be most likely to take issue with him, of course, is over his assertion that 'criticism as knowledge' is somehow different from this general condition.

Macherey, like so many other critics and theorists, first divides literary from non-literary uses of language, but often retains a fundamental distinction in his writing between books that are worthy of serious study and books that are not. One way of formulating this latter distinction is to say that the co-presence of contradictory discources is what makes the text interesting. One example that he offers is that of a book which almost self-consciously gets its facts about 'the real world' wrong, but neverthe-less has an internal logic and development which means that it possesses its own version of plausibility.

This plausibility, though, is of a kind which is unique to literary texts. These differ from other uses of language, not in respect of the words that they use or the style in which they are written, but by virtue of the fact that they lack a referent. All language activity consists of a momentary distanc-ing of the speaker from the object spoken about (the thing after all cannot be present in the word itself) but literature has this curious feature of not actually making direct reference to the everyday world at all. By seeming, in purely formal terms, exactly like other non-literary uses of language, but differing from them in this one vital feature, they become, in effect, parodic versions of ordinary language usage. It is this quality of parody about them which enables them to make visible the presence of ideology within text.

Many traditional critiques of literary works have treated unity as a feature to be praised in them. This is also the case with the classic structuralist approaches, which aimed to discover a unity of narrative purpose and direction behind the disparate surface elements of narrative flow. Macherey, in contrast, finds this apparent unity to be spurious, a further example of that pervasive organic mataphor in which the book develops just as a plant develops from a seed. In contrast, he stresses that literary production is work, and resembles other forms of work in that it consists of the combining together of various and disparate elements. It is not just the releasing of something that was already there (there is an old story about the sculptor who was told 'How clever of you to know that Mr Lincoln was in the middle of that lump of rock'); nor is it the magical conjuring trick of suddenly producing something that was not there a moment ago—a secular equivalent of transubstantiation.

The writer works to produce his text under determinate social condi-tions. What goes into it is therefore to a degree constrained, but the writer has also a degree of freedom within which to operate. Were it not so, after all, the end of a story would be apparent as soon as we began to read it. This degree of freedom enables the writer to amuse himself as well as us; Macherey therefore terms him the first reader of his own work.

There are two further points to be noted about the relative freedom within which the writer operates. One is that the various ISAs can interact one with another. The intervention that consists of writing a book can therefore have consequences, for example, within the field of other ideologies—such as that of schooling. It used to be believed, for example, that Dickens's individual and willed intervention in describing Dotheboys Hall in *Nicholas Nickeleby* had been solely instrumental in obtaining the closure of such establishments. More detailed research later showed that a variety of social and economic factors was involved in this process. Collapse of story. However, if we envisage Dickens as operating within one ideology to bring about changes within another, and if we see his narrative as partly but not wholly determined by where it is situated, and the various forms of struggle by which it is surrounded, then perhaps this more modest role can be judged to have been actually carried out.

The other point to be noted about this anecdote is that it relates to more than just ideology, however. The running of schools is an economic activity of some significance, and if ideological interventions can affect this then we are looking at an example of superstructure bringing about changes in the base. It is critical not to overstate this claim—to produce a list of 'Ten Books that Changed the World'—or we finish up with absurd claims such as that the Middle Ages ended because everybody suddenly started reading the Bible. Nevertheless, Macherey's position, if it does not permit literature to win any major wars, still, unlike 'Dialectical Materialism', allows it to run a few guerrilla campaigns with some success.

However, to write in this way is to run the risk once more of seeming to assert that books bear messages which a waiting world can receive. Macherey's position is rather different. Books are written in everyday language, which is the language of illusion and ideology. Because they do not actually perpetrate an illusion, however—after all, we know that they are not 'true'—they provide a representation of ideology. But this representation is not some fruit that will just drop into our mouths if we stand looking at it; it has to be studied, worked over, and this is the role of criticism as knowledge. 'A theory of literary production must show us what the text "knows", how it "knows"' (1966, p. 64).

Macherey cautions us against various activities. One is evaluative criticism of the kind that holds the work up against some external model of achievement, and comments, in effect, 'Six out of ten; could try harder'. This is to assume that there is some ideal book which lies somewhere further on than this one: a metaphysical assumption that Macherey explicitly rejects. Another is the kind of interpretive reading that assumes there is a meaning in there waiting to be discovered, like the motto inside the cracker. For Macherey there is both more and less meaning in the book than this. 'A proper investigation ... takes as its object that hollow speech which the work utters so discreetly; it measures the *distance* which separates the *various* meanings' (pp. 78–9).

Just as for Kristeva, the book is riddled with intertextuality, with all the constellations of meanings to be found in other texts; there are the everyday discussions in which we find the same discourses which turn up in the work; and, finally, there is whatever the book is actually incapable of saying, just like a patient under analysis reaching to express what his very condition makes inexpressible. This is the hollowness that Macherey finds at the centre of the work. It is important to remember, though, that it is the work which is being analysed, not the author.

There is a whole set of meanings here, then, but it is not an infinite set. Criticizing the Italian scholar Umberto Eco for adopting a position somewhat similar to that of Fish outlined earlier, Macherey insists that the set of possible reader-generated meanings may be infinite, but the set of scientifically-warranted, textually-located meanings is distinctly finite.

Because the text does not say everything, there remains the task for the critic of saying something else; 'after another fashion' (p. 82), Macherey adds. His discourse is therefore more than a supplement, but less than a deconstruction. It retains, in discussing the distribution of discourses and of power, the privileged position of rational and analytical thought. This was 1966. By 1983 Macherey's definition of the nature of the activity involved had changed and developed somewhat. His opposition to 'Dialectical Materialism', as described earlier, had led him further along the path of rejecting any absolute notion of truth in favour of the alternative criterion of appropriateness. Lurking in the background here we can perhaps detect the shades of Nietzsche and Foucault. He finds, both in the practice of philosophy, and in those practices that philosophy investigates, the competing forces of materialism and idealism, and, since the various elements of the situation are variously determined, he maintains that it is a kind of metaphysical fantasy to assume that one philosophy from one era can be compared with another from another to determine which provides the truer description. The implication of all this, as I take it, is that 'criticism as knowledge' is as situated as any other discourse, as subject to the ceaseless wear and tear of dialectical pressures running through history:

> The disorder at the level of its own organization that is caused by the reproduction of a thought in an objective setting other than that in which it was originally elaborated is not accidental; rather it brings out whatever is most particular in its working order.   (1983, pp. 149–50)

One of the characteristic errors of 'Dialectical Materialism', as Macherey sees it, is that it is fundamentally teleological in its structures: that is to say, it represents the events of history as working towards some foreknowable goal or end point. For Macherey, in contrast, history is 'in the last analysis, struggles, relations of power, issues at stake, the detail of whose interplay no knowledge can predict' (ibid, p. 152). At this point, it seems to me, Foucault takes one step further out of the shadows.

It is as well, in comparing the earlier with the later Macherey, to be quite clear that in his earlier book he was specifically discussing the

practice of literary analysis, whereas in his 1983 essay he was talking of the
practice of philosophy. Nevertheless, I hope I have done enough to
establish that the two activities are sufficiently similar, within his writings,
in the ways in which they investigate phenomena and create the domain
within which to investigate them, for comments about the one to be
applicable to the other. It is therefore highly appropriate, I would suggest,
to consider the following passage in this light:

> What we learn from a philosophy's posthumous history is that it is not
> complete at the moment when it is to all appearances concluded, because
> its author has written in the last word, since its real destiny, its historical
> becoming, it that it should continue to work itself out, while at the same
> time decomposing itself in the complex concatenation of the alien dis-
> courses which take it as their object and which cast an ever-novel light
> upon its content.   (1983, pp. 150–1)

One of the interesting things about that sentence is that it would probably
be possible to mask out the word 'philosophy', show the result to informed
readers, invite them to complete the blank, and obtain responses that
would divide between 'a novel' and 'literary criticism'. It has frequently
been said of writers such as Nietzsche and Derrida that they obliterate the
dividing line between literary composition and philosophical discourse; it
is interesting to find the same phenomenon in the work of such a rigorous
Marxist.

Just as philosophy and literary analysis are not uniquely privileged, in
any epistemological sense, as forms of discourse, so it cannot be main-
tained that they automatically lead to any uniquely differentiated form of
action in and upon the real world. In an essay jointly written with Étienne
Balibar in 1978, Macherey refers to the Marxist expectation that Marxist
philosophy should not only comment upon the world, but should also
change it. However, they point out that it is perfectly possible to substitute
a Marxist set of theories for a bourgeois set—in other words, to create a
sort of spurious Marxist aesthetic—and yet leave the practical relationship both of individuals and of classes to works of art in exactly the same
state.

What is therefore needed, they argue, is a proper understanding of the
way in which literature, as an institution, interacts with other institutions
such as a national education policy and a national language, whilst
retaining at the same time its own specific features and identity. The
national language, often described as a unifying force, provides in fact a
misleading appearance of unity which masks differing class experiences
and class goals. The notion of a national literature, a canon of great works,
is itself largely a product of the educational system, which has to constitute such a body of works before it can, with any appearance of
rationality, proceed to teach them. They therefore see the education
system as a whole functioning in two stages. The first, at the level of
primary education, consists of ensuring that every pupil is proficient in the

national language, and is thereby incorporated into the unifying ideology (or ideology of unification) that operates in this area. The second, at the advanced secondary stage of education, consists of a kind of initiation into the community of those declared competent to handle literature proper. At the first stage the teaching process concentrates on correctness of usage and the ability to produce simple, functional writing. Further on in the educational system comes an introduction to literary style, and an induction into the skills of producing it.

It is important to note that at no stage of this process are local variants or regional norms of language included, since these would make manifest the disparate nature of the school population within the country as a whole. The contradiction in practice falls within a different sphere, so that pupils are taught both that the language is a common inheritance, and that mastery of literary texts is a specific skill which only some of them will acquire.

By these means the bourgeois ideology of schooling both constitutes its subjects (the school pupils) within the process of schooling, and overtly maintains that literature is the product in each case of an individual genius and characterized by the unique style of that particular author. Whilst in fact structuring a whole society, in rhetoric it maintains that people are separate, autonomous, unique individuals, a few of whom happen to be literary geniuses, and rather more of whom become competent readers of literature.

If literature, as a social institution, is as deeply implicated as this in the perpetuation of bourgeois ideology, then, according to the argument of Macherey and Balibar, it can't simply pull itself up by its own bootstraps, mend its ways, and detach itself from the dominant ideology. If it did so, then, by definition, it would no longer be literature, at least as we know it. As things stand it has a fundamental role in the reproduction of social relations—that is to say, in their transfer from the members of one generation to those of another. Though literature may be the same to all readers in the sense that it is the same black marks on the page that are being studied, for some, those destined for the positions of power and control within society, it arrives as a confirmation of their privileged status, and their initiation into the skills of reading it is an enactment rather than a mere representation of their adoption of positions of power. Though it is a process that they have to submit to, at that time, this is a little like saying that a king submits to being crowned. For the majority, those destined for inferior positions within society; the books may, up to a point at least, be the same, but the experience of encountering them is very different. Since these books are demarcated as requiring a skill in composition that very few possess, and since reading them with any fluency is something that only a portion of the population is induced to aspire to, social differentiation, of the grossest kind, is built into the texts themselves as an inextricable part of their composition.

In responding to these assertions it is as well to remember both the similarities and the differences between the British and French educational systems, and between English and French literature. In both countries common schooling is a feature of the early years, and social differentiation is increasingly visible within the upper years of the system. To that extent there seems little reason to suppose that a comment that is valid in respect of one system is inapplicable to another. The language of French literature, though semantically and syntactically very close to spoken French, does however have certain characteristic features, such as a form of past tense rarely found outside books, which mark it off from other forms of discourse. It is a little as though, to read English literature, students had to become acquainted with the few oddities of Shakespearian English (differentiation of singular and plural in the second person, 'it' for 'its' as a possessive adjective, etc.) and they then went on to meet these same features in Dickens and William Golding. Because of this, it is not as contradictory as it might seem for Macherey to claim both that literature is, in respect of the great majority of its utterances, indistinguishable from other usages of speech, and that the comprehension and use of literary French amounts to a skill that pupils typically acquire only through the educational system.

Where it may seem that there is some difference between the experiences of the two countries, though, is in the ideology of pedagogy, and this is an issue that we shall return to in a later chapter. It would be as well to remember at this point, however, that the conjunction of common schooling, common national language, and common ideology is something frequently aimed at, and perhaps often achieved, in this country. The Newbolt Report (1921), commenting on what it saw as universal French pride in the national language, such that even an artisan would object that an expression 'is not French', went on to say that 'Such a feeling for our own native language would be a bond of union between classes, and would beget the right kind of national pride' (p. 22). Appreciation of fine style and noble thinking, it continued, were to be found in all classes as a norm rather than an exception, though this sensibility was easily discouraged by 'unfavourable circumstances'. It would be only a few individuals who would go on to develop technical expertise in the subject, but all those who were capable of experiencing enjoyment at anything other than the merely sensuous level would continue to find, in the way in which literature reflected life at its best, a shared enjoyment. At which point, Macherey might feel inclined to add, he rests his case.

I began this chapter by indicating that it was profitable to compare various aspects of Macherey's work with that of Foucault. I should now like to end it by saying that, if power is always met by resistance, then one ideology can, and perhaps typically does, encounter opposition from another, even if the two are not equally matched. It would be a great disservice to Macherey to imply that he was some kind of neo-functionalist, and that his notion of reproduction was in some way equivalent to a set of checks and balances within society. On the contrary, he is perpetually reminding us that literature, and specifically the institution of literature within schools, is the site of struggle. Though education and literature are yoked together in a powerful team, other forces pull in other directions. Indeed, if they did not, it might be argued, it would be surprising if any society went to the difficulty and expense of investing in a universal education system of the kind we know.

6 Literary theory in classroom practice

There is no dearth of narrowly utilitarian pedagogies ready to declare that there is no particular need for a place for the study of literature within an educational curriculum at all. The fact that such assertions frequently co-exist in practice with other assertions that it is the duty of teachers of literature to instil certain core values should occasion no particular surprise, since heavily charged ideological utterances frequently display logical inconsistencies of this kind. The problem of coping with such contradictions, however, becomes a practical one for those whose work depends upon refuting such statements. The difficulty, though, lies in deciding upon what ground to mount a counter-attack. Since the reasons for teachers wishing to teach literature are frequently couched in moral terms themselves, it often seems as though a number of vital points are ceded at the outset.

The reasons advanced by the representatives of the State for the teaching of English as a part of the core curriculum, from the Newbolt Report onwards, relate to the establishing of a sense of national identity and of shared values. The reasons offered by many radical teachers relate to the establishing of a community of experiences and of shared values. The two justifications are embarrassingly similar. Variations on either side of this norm, though, pose as many problems as they solve. A greater concentration upon the pupil as subject, and upon the processes of human growth and development, can readily come to appear an apologia for liberal individualism. A defence of the uniqueness of the English literary tradition, and of its capacity to focus and articulate dissent, founders both upon the intractability of some of the material and upon the fact that this alternative comes to resemble the original State-sponsored version rather too closely. Leavis's 'We were Cambridge in spite of

Cambridge' begins to sound like Chesterton's 'We are the people of England, and we have not spoken yet'.

In part this can be held to be a matter of which works are thought worthy of study, and for what reasons. Perhaps the most notorious 'classic' example during this century has been that of Milton, praised originally by gentlemanly scholars for the grandeur of his style, its latinate periods providing a functional equivalent for Virgil's *Aeneid* as a cultural foundation-myth, then condemned by Eliot and Leavis for having introduced a dissociation of sensibility into literary English, then reinstated (largely by historians such as Hill and Thompson) on the strength of his revolutionary credentials. It requires a cool head to remember that it is the same poet, and the same poems, that are being discussed in all these instances. And Milton is not unique in receiving this treatment; to take examples of more recent writing, Lawrence is assimilated into the liberal humanist tradition despite the mass of wildly contradictory evidence to be found throughout his writings, and Orwell's *Animal Farm* is smoothly inserted into the educational system as an unambiguous denunciation of communism by One Who Has Been There and Knows. The history of these examples should be a powerful warning for anyone inclined to believe too readily that a work of literature is a shell from which one single and unambiguous meaning can be extracted.

However, it is not only representatives of high culture within a context of national sponsorship that find their stock rising and falling in this fashion. The history of CSE English, with the opportunities it has provided for individual schools to select works to be studied for various forms of assessment, has yet to be written in full. However, though it will doubtless show examples of innovation that have extended to a considerable degree the range of texts thought to be examination-worthy, it will probably also reveal that effective control over what is deemed acceptable is not greatly diminished by being made more diffuse. So, though the texts may change, the meanings that are derived from them do not alter greatly.

Perhaps, therefore, we should propose our own version of the rallying-cry 'Back to basics!' and try to examine just what justifications can be offered for just what kinds of practices within the scope of the English lesson. I should emphasize that, in what follows, I am adopting a fairly eclectic approach to the theories examined in the first part of the book. As it happens, my comments roughly follow the order of my earlier presentation, but in practice a lot of what I am describing would be characterized by overlap.

In Chapter Two I quoted Barthes as asserting that use of narrative and response to narrative were fundamental human attributes. There seems, on the basis of the available evidence, no reason to doubt this, so long as we remember that what people go on to do with narratives can vary as much as the languages in which they are couched. In view of this, it would be as malign to rob children of the experience of narrative as it would be to deprive them of the experience of using language. However, though instances of both forms of deprivation are documented, they require an atypical control of the learning environment before they can be put into effect. A more typical situation is one in which the child enters the system of formal education as an experienced and, to a degree, sophisticated consumer and originator of narrative. Again, this is something which it is difficult to quantify, but it seems reasonable to suppose that exposure to radio and television transmissions, to audio and video recordings, to reading material of various kinds, and to the normal interchange of conversation, all ensure that exposure to narrative is at least as great as it would be in many cultures that rely purely on oral methods of transmission.

Not only is the exposure quantitively great, but the narrative devices that are to be found within it are tolerably sophisticated as well. An ordinary five-minute cartoon film on teatime television can yield examples of analepsis and intercalated narrative sufficient to keep narratologists busy for some time, and on the whole these devices do not seem to lead to problems of comprehension for young viewers. In many respects, then, schools might feel themselves entitled to assume that their pupils already have at least a nodding acquaintance with the proairetic code of *S/Z* even before lessons begin.

These comments apply to the reception of narrative, and, like other aspects of language skills, the capacity for production lags a good way behind. There is therefore every reason for schools to mount as comprehensive a programmme as possible in order to develop a child's capacity to generate narrative, and this programme should aim to develop oral as well as written skills, in order that narrative ability should not be confused with orthographic capability.

However, the fact that a child exhibits competence as a receiver of narrative does not mean that this is a conscious skill, and one of the goals for a programme of narrative study during the early years of schooling should be to enable pupils to comment as much as possible on the structure of stories to which they are exposed. Comments such as 'What do you think is going to happen next?', followed by the supplementary 'And why do you think that?' provide pupils with the opportunity, not available elsewhere, to begin to specify, from within their own terminology, the basic units of narrative development. Prediction is one skill involved; another is retrospective analysis. Here I have in mind questions such as 'Did you guess that Pooh was going to get stuck in the rabbit hole?' 'What might have made us think that this was going to happen?' If Barthes is right in asserting that the logical fallacy *post hoc, ergo propter hoc* is the foundation stone of narrative, then we need to be able to read this formula both forwards and backwards, both in order to follow what is going on in narrative and, later, to see that this *is* a logical fallacy, and one that can be avoided by conscious effort.

So far the comments I have been making on reading skills all relate to the lowest of Barthes' three levels of narrative structure. The other basic skill that is involved is of course the ability to read upwards from narrative flow towards the level of discourse. The most typical feature here will be the indexing of character by incidents that occur at the level of plot, but this leads on with a seeming inevitability to questions of relationships and the establishment of norms. Here the kinds of questions I have in mind are ones like 'How does the Queen of Hearts treat her gardeners?' 'What kind of a person do you think she is?' 'Does Alice sound like someone who is speaking to a queen?' 'Was it right for her to talk to the Queen in this way?' 'Is she polite or rude to other grown-up creatures that she meets in the story?' 'Do you suppose that we are expected to approve of this or not?'

Where narrative structure is concerned, it can also be a mistake to assume that all the various types of narrative categorized by Genette will be encountered in totally unstructured reading and viewing. I have already suggested that analepsis and intercalated narrative are frequently to be met with, but other features, such as iterative and repetitive narration, might have to be more consciously incorporated into a reading scheme. I should emphasize that this would be done, not on the principle of climbing Mount Everest because it is there, but because without it some of the more interesting and rewarding books for further study cannot be coped with as successfully.

The last of my suggested questions on *Alice in Wonderland* leads us effectively into a consideration of the role of the implied reader in the study of narratives. In Chapter Three I discussed this within the context of reception theory and reader-response theory, but by now it may be more satisfactory to consider this as a product of the dominant ideological discourse within a text. Not, I hasten to add, that this would be announced as the ostensible subject of the lesson to a class of ten-year-olds. Nevertheless, there is quite a case to be made for the assertion that by this age a curriculum should be introducing pupils to texts with very different intended audiences from the one currently reading them. There used to be a consensus around the notion that, since literature provided access, of a fairly direct kind, to the sensuous reality to which it referred, pupils should be given books about different times and different places— literature as the Complete Home Traveller. In a way I am proposing a variant on this, saying that the classroom should resonate to as many different discourses as possible. Geographical variation is not, it must be admitted, very relevant to what I am suggesting, but historical and social variation is. Considerable co-ordination is therefore called for between teachers of English and those of social studies, and in this regard the traditional distinctions between literary and non-literary texts have little that is useful to offer.

It may well seem that I am only describing an existing state of affairs. After all, it is more than twenty years since the use of source books came to play a considerable part in English lessons, and the use of facsimilies of original documents during history lessons has at least as long a pedigree. There is a distinction, though, since both these forms of anthologizing were mostly organized on thematic lines, whereas what I am proposing is a collation of material not on the grounds of overt subject but on the basis of more covert presuppositions.

Though I have been discussing a convergence between English and social studies, I am by no means proposing a merger. Fiction after all remains deviant discourse—its use of the pronoun system wilfully failing to correspond to that of the actual participants in the speech event—and, in relation to normal utterances, it retains what Macherey calls its parodic quality, resembling them in form but not in function. This visibility of its fabrication is not something to be lightly thrown away. In a sense, therefore, I am not so much suggesting that literature should be treated as an adjunct of history as proposing that historical documents should be treated somewhat as though they are literary works themselves, judged, as Foucault suggested, not on their truth value but in respect of the effects they were designed to produce upon others. Power as mediated and expressed through language can form a unifying theme in work in this area.

However, in drawing attention to the capacity of texts to transmit and reproduce ideology, I am by no means suggesting that this should be represented as an automatic process leading to a foregone conclusion. Foucault, after all, stressed that power was characterized and defined by resistance, and Macherey saw literature as traversed by various discourses rather than dominated by one single monolithic one. What this means in practice for teaching is that interventions are possible, and are possibly effective.

And it is not only the teacher that can bring about this intervention. The activities that pupils carry out in consuming or analysing texts are perhaps more various than these two labels suggest, and perhaps also not as mutually exclusive. The capacity to respond to narrative is presumably an aspect of consumption, but the ludic aspects of this process that Barthes emphasizes amount to more than mere passivity. When a pupil is constructing in her head various meanings for a poem, rejecting some, gaining pleasure from pressing other towards an absurd conclusion, holding two in suspension as alternative possibilities, she is carrying out an activity that warrants more recognition than a lot of literary theory is normally prepared to accord to her. Just as the author is the first reader of what he has written, so the actual reader, approaching a text for the first time, becomes, so to speak, its first re-writer. After all, since no narrative really carries its end inscribed in its beginning, the active process of speculation and anticipation, the 'what if's and 'probably's, amount to a testing out of the conditions and determinants of possibility. The writer's possibilities, we can recognize, are not co-extensive with the readers', but there may be an element of overlap nonetheless.

It is from this process of anticipation and speculation that an awareness of ideological activity within a text can develop; it does not have to grow from completely different roots. Just as a text can be interrogated to try to establish what it is about to say, so it can be pressed on what it is saying in coded terms, or is skirting round saying altogether. Some people would want to argue that 'Literature' should have a privileged place within the curriculum; others, that other literatures, such as working-class auto-biographies, women's writing, black writing, should join it or supplant it. There is indeed a powerful case to be made out for at least the second of these possibilities, but there is also a danger that such a rewriting of the syllabus will simply reinstate the old fallacy that such newcomers will breeze into the classroom bringing with them the authorial experiences in which they were grounded in all their sensuous direct immediacy. This book has tried to establish a case for believing that such a trust is misplaced, that literature does not provide direct access to objects or experiences, that the bond between signifier and signified is as loose as an escapologist's handcuffs, that the past cannot be re-lived.

Blake wrote of seeing the world in a grain of sand. By the same token, then, are we to assume that the contradictions of an era of late capitalism can be made manifest by a study of any appropriately chosen work of 'Literature'? It is interesting to step back a little, and see how much this argument resembles the earlier claim that a study of the debased language of modern advertising, plus a close reading of a few major works of the Great Tradition, will tell us all we need to know about the corruption of modern civilization and the values that can be pitted against it. It is easy to mock both enterprises for overweening ambition, but it is useful also to consider how attractive their optimism appears when set against the assertion that the educational system will do neither more nor less than reproduce the inequalities of society from generation to generation.

Even if our ambition should be tinged with modesty, then, there is no reason to suppose that our approach to classic, or not-so-classic, texts should be over-coloured with reverence. To illustrate some of the pos-sibilities I have in mind, I propose shortly to look again at *The Adventures of Tom Sawyer*, the book that I used earlier to illustrate various aspects of narratological terminology. What I should like to do now is to consider how it might be approached as a possible book for study in the lower years of secondary education. Before starting on this enterprise, however, I should point out that here, as elsewhere in this book, I have worked with perfectly conventional reading choices drawn from within a very settled middle-class tradition of respectable writing for children. The principal reason for doing so is that my chosen examples should be familiar to as wide a potential readership as possible, but it is also important to recog-nize that in doing so I am contributing in a small way to the reinforcement of their position as established works. It does indeed sometimes seem, however, as though it is only the theories that keep changing, whereas the books stay the same.

I stated in the previous paragraph that *Tom Sawyer* was a piece of respectable writing for children, and so for all practical purposes it is, and has been effectively throughout over a century. However, one of its many interesting features is that its central character is someone who operates at the margins of respectability, cherishes and disseminates fantasies of lawlessness, and adopts as his chief ally a boy, Huckleberry Finn, who is definitely beyond the pale of any civilized company. Huck, of course, is in due course to become the protagonist of a separate book, and one that has for a long time been recognized as the more productive for analysis of various kinds.

But *Tom Sawyer* can offer us plenty to be getting on with. The opening chapters reveal him as someone who can convert his punishments into profits, as in the famous sequence in which he puts out to tender his 'right' to whitewash the fence. As a narrative this typically has considerable attraction, and the values to which it variously appeals are sufficiently incongruously juxtaposed to be easily commented upon. The tissue of small lies, thefts, and deceits for which Tom is punished are connived at or excused, as is his commercial initiative in sub-contracting the punishment he is set. The question can therefore be put: is commercial initiative in effect equated with lying, thieving, and deceiving? If the same skills are required for both, where does that leave the 'respectable' adult figures who appear in the story?

Since it is open to us to interrogate the narrative, and to observe what it does not say as well as what it does, we can then go on to list those figures that appear in the book, and consider how representative or otherwise they may be of the community at large as it would have been found in Twain's own childhood. The categories that are present seem to me to amount to the following: children; women who are presumably living on some form of unearned income, large or small (Aunt Polly, Widow Douglas); salaried representatives of minor authority who are there to be mocked and teased (the schoolmaster, the clergyman); derelicts, drop-outs, and other socially marginalized figures (Muff Potter, Injun Joe, and Huck himself in this respect); and, crucially, two representatives of the fee-earning or salaried professional intelligentsia, distinguished from their lesser brethren by their capacity for effective action for good or ill (Judge Thatcher, Doctor Robinson). Self-employed workers have at best walk-on parts, such as the old Welshman and his (unnamed) sons; and hired hands appear only (but significantly enough) in disembodied ways such as a voice overhead on the ferryboat at night.

Who is missing? Girls, in any capacity other than a purely passive one in relation to initiatives undertaken by boys. Women who work, either as employers or employed; the narrative is unable to make anything of Tom's cousin Mary, who vanishes after the opening chapters. Women who are currently married; Mrs Thatcher, lacking any ferrous element in her character, swoons away immediately she has made her only major appearance. Men who are engaged in any industrial or commercial activity. Slaves; Jim, who is to play a major part in *Huckleberry Finn*, makes the briefest of appearances here.

There is then a paradox which is fundamental to the whole narrative.

On the face of it, Tom is engaged in a series of more or less tolerated revolts against the trammels and expectations of the society he lives in. Yet the book itself is no *Middlemarch*, providing, in however abbreviated a form, a token demonstration of the existence of all categories of inhabitants. On the contrary, its significance lies in the fact that authority is made visible only in the easily circumvented figures of aged aunt, ridiculous schoolmaster and inattentive preacher. Effectively, the locus of power within the community is never made manifest.

It is important to emphasize what is not being said here. Macherey took care to reject the notion of literature as reflection; this was what 'Dialectical Materialism' expected of fiction—a direct representation of the composition of a society, coupled with strategies which endorsed its more progressive elements. Such a representation is not being offered here, certainly, and it would be difficult to locate Tom in the vanguard of anything. But the strategy that I am offering is rather different: to identify the contradictions, gaps, and silences within the text; to get some idea of the contradictions of the historical American society within which it was composed; and, finally, to see what contradictions arise when these two structures are juxtaposed. This is the kind of project for which I envisage an active collaboration between English and social studies departments, and my comments at this point in the book are intended to highlight the major themes which an effective teaching strategy can be designed to elicit.

Tom becomes rich; this is the key event in the novel. The riches that he acquires have been collected together by Injun Joe as the outcomes of various illegal acts, of which we know of burglary and grave-robbing. Injun Joe's principal crime, however, is the murder of the doctor who hired him to procure a cadaver. All these crimes have parodic versions in Tom's activities. He organizes his friends to play pirates; by means of innumerable childhood superstitions, he has dealings with ghosts, spirits, and other apparitions from beyond the grave; when it comes to murder, he brings about, not once but twice, his own apparent death. The significance of this shift from murder to apparent suicide is something I shall want to return to later, but for the present it is enough to notice how closely his activities parallel those of his persecutor/victim. The one significant modification, however, is that whereas Injun Joe in all seriousness buries his ill-gotten gains, Tom conducts a mock hunt for hidden treasure, the ironic futility of which parodically indicates that Injun Joe's digging and delving is, eventually, equally purposeless.

Many readers of the story find that there is insufficient psychological motivation provided for the murder that takes place in the churchyard. Injun Joe refers to an incident five years previously when the Robinson family refused him food at their door, and had him jailed as a vagrant. He then starts a fight, in the course of which the doctor is killed. In terms of the structure of the story, however, the significance seems clear enough. Robinson, notionally a pillar of the local community, is breaking both the law and powerful taboos in bringing the dead back above ground. Yet he is doing so, it has to be presumed, in order to increase his professional knowledge by carrying out an illicit dissection. The morality of success and initiative within his chosen area of activity is as deeply questionable as was Tom's in relation to the fence; in each case social norms approve the ends (profit, knowledge) whilst treating the means as deeply questionable.

Injun Joe's attack upon the doctor is the revenge of the dispossessed and the outcast; his activity in this respect stands in stark contrast to Huck's total lack of aggression throughout. At the time that the deed is recounted in the story, Injun Joe is accorded some grounds for feeling aggrieved, yet sympathy for him is instantly qualified by his own statement that his capacity to sustain a grudge is derived from the Indian blood that is in him. This reference, brief though it is, both cues in the recollection of the larger dispossession of his people, and at the same time neutralizes any moral indignation by its racialist assumption that to bear a grudge so long is the mark of a morally degenerate being. I listed earlier the various categories of people not represented in this story; the Indians, the indigenous inhabitants of the area, are the most powerfully over-determined absence, perhaps, in the whole story. Complementary work in social studies should therefore aim to highlight just what the population of the area would have consisted of, and how this distribution would have been arrived at.

Injun Joe's triumph is not a lasting one. Forced into concealment once his guilt is made known, he disguises himself as a Spaniard (one alien masking himself as another) and is forced to move his person and his treasure from pillar to post. Finally his death occurs unnoticed in the aftermath of, and as a consequence of, Tom's disappearance and quasi-miraculous return, and Tom, by right of discovery, acquires half Injun Joe's wealth. The outcast halfbreed's assault upon society therefore results in the establishment of a poor white boy as a potential recruit to the dominant grouping within society; a negation of a negation, indeed. Macherey, in Althusserian vein, pointed out that a text can know more than it says, and say more than it knows.

What I have been trying to do here is to map out some of the themes that seem to me to be significant, and some of the ways in which a teacher can catalogue them in the course of lesson preparation. Clearly I am not suggesting that the ostensible content of a lesson should follow precisely the same path. Nevertheless, the fact that the narrative, at various critical points, allows these issues to be raised does mean that it is possible to give them a reasonably adequate treatment. When Injun Joe dies, or when Tom acquires the treasure, many readers are brought up short and forced to examine their own reactions, which can include pity or surprise. It is at these points that a good teaching strategy can begin to elicit some of the issues that I have mentioned.

One other probable feature of the classroom is that half of the occupants of it will be girls. I have already indicated that both girls and women within the narrative are presented entirely in relation to the care and attention that they dedicate to boys and men. Aunt Polly and Mary are there to serve Tom; Mrs Thatcher to look after the Judge and his daughter. Becky, during sequences such as the visit to the caves discussed in some detail earlier, undertakes no initiatives of her own and, significantly, the only time the narrative enables her to start a sequence is in the privileged area of coquetry in the schoolyard. Even this, though, does not in the end constitute an independent area of activity, since Tom is able to outscheme her and bring her flirtatious behaviour round to ensure a more perfect submission to himself.

Once she has submitted, though, what can the narrative then do with her? She is described as attractive, but the conventions that are being observed permit of nothing more than hand-holding to ensue from this attraction. The problem is, at one level, solved by the mock-wedding that results from the shared eating of the cake in the cave, but the marriage is not, so to speak, consummated after the pair have emerged into the daylight once more. Indeed, the really significant interaction here, as I have suggested earlier, is between Tom and the Judge, when the boy's insertion into the adult framework of power is being mapped out for him. Becky, it is interesting to note, does not reappear in *Huckleberry Finn*, since until Tom reaches adulthood (which is perpetually deferred) neither he nor the narrative has any further use for her, and she cannot, after all, constitute an independent focus of interest. Indeed, were she ever to become a married woman she would be just as null a figure as is her mother.

Conclusions such as these give offence, and it is right that they should. What might have seemed obvious within the conventions of a nineteenth-century readership now instead appears blatant. Since the narrative provides Becky with such a circumscribed role, it constitutes a double challenge to a present-day readership. One part of this consists of an attempt to define the degree to which the conventions of literature, and of society, currently allow women to be more independent agents than Becky ever was. The other, and perhaps more important, challenge is to recognize the degree to which the situation remains the same.

One way into this issue is therefore to ask the question of how the work gets done during the course of this novel. The domestic work that is shown taking place is entirely and directly child-centred: mending clothes, checking that children have washed properly, and so on. Other activities, such as cooking and cleaning, take place offstage. Despite the fact that this is a slave-owning society, no slave labour occurs during the course of the narrative. And, as I have pointed out earlier, no manufacture, transport, or trade takes place either.

To draw attention to these absences is, from certain kinds of traditional viewpoint, to lay oneself open to the charge of purely negative criticism, of pretending to know more about that particular riparian community than a man who grew up there, of harbouring a secret wish to write the novel

oneself whilst lacking the ability to do so. I have already suggested that
negativity may well be regarded as a virtue, and I have proposed that work
within the social studies area of the curriculum, such as a project on
America before and after the Civil War, would yield both historical and
ideological material of the greatest interest. As for the wish to re-write the
novel, that, in effect, can be the best outcome of all. If pupils can be led to
speculate on what kind of a book, or what kind of a world, it would be if the
Beckys were the ones to choose the schoolyard friends or to find the route
out of the cave, then surely we have a beneficial educational outcome,
ratified both by reader-response theory and by more rigorous forms of
analysis, which no talk of the integrity of the text should be allowed to
prevent.

7 Further theory and teaching

In my comments on *Tom Sawyer* up to this point I have been looking at some of the work that I consider could profitably be done with the text in the relatively junior years of secondary schooling. What I shall now move on to consider are some of the ways in which it can be used in sixth forms, or even in introductory courses in universities, to illustrate some further aspects of literary theory.

In the previous chapter, I indicated that an interesting substitution occurred when Tom, paralleling the crimes committed by Injun Joe, staged a pretend suicide instead of the murder that Joe carries out in reality. At a purely naturalistic level, this is a very curious activity, and it is given some plausibility only by the implication that Tom feels himself unjustly persecuted, and wishes to prove to himself that the adult world will indeed truly feel sorry when he is gone. The event that brings matters to a head is a snub that he receives from Becky, after which he begins '"going on" like an Indian'—a phrase that underscores his identification with lawlessness. He and his two friends therefore take themselves off to an uninhabited island in the river, arranging for the world to believe that they have been drowned.

Tom is an orphan, and his life is therefore characterized by a lack of parents, if not of quasi-parental care. It is also marked by poverty, even if the simplicity of his home life is somewhat softened by a quality of reminiscence in the telling of it. Parents and plenty are therefore the two most significant gaps in his life. On the other hand, the island teems with life and abundance. Fish more or less beg to be caught, and turtle eggs are to be found, fifty or sixty at a time, by scooping up the sand by the water's edge. There is also the added attraction of Huck's corn-cob pipes, which they have to learn to draw on with moderation.

The French psychologist Jacques Lacan (1977), in an influential re-working of Freudian principles, termed the early, pre-Oedipal phase of a child's existence the imaginary. In this stage the bond between child and mother is deep and intense, gratification is typically immediate, and the child has no clear sense either of a division between himself and the mother, or of a stable ego identity of his own. Deprived of this experience at an early age, and nourishing feelings of rejection by his world, Tom is in effect staging a retreat to the primal unity and gratification of which he was bereft. He crosses the stream to get to the place where the eggs come from. Huck is similarly a motherless boy. Joe Harper, the third member of the party, does have a mother, but she has just punished him for drinking some cream—an accusation which he denies. The pattern of a guilty return to the primal sources of sustenance is therefore complete.

For Lacan the imaginary comes to an end with the mirror-stage, in which the child, still not able perfectly to co-ordinate the various parts of his own body, receives from a mirror, or from some other aspect of the environment, an image of himself that is whole, integrated, complete. Realizing that that image is him, he proceeds to identify with it, to accept the way in which he will be inserted into the adult world which crucially depends for its structure upon the separateness of persons, and upon a grammar of relationships which permits certain combinations and excludes others.

For the three boys on the island, this experience comes when they watch the steamer drift past, firing shot over the water, in observance of a local superstition, to make the supposed dead bodies rise to the surface of the water. They speculate as to who may be the objects of this search.

> Presently a revealing thought flashed through Tom's mind, and he exclaimed: 'Boys, I know who's drowned; it's us!'   (p. 98)

This recognition, I suggest, is for Tom a mirror-stage, presenting to him an image of himself and how the world may see him—'They felt like heroes on the instant', the text continues. From here onward the sojourn on the island had no more point, and Tom embarks upon a staged return to the community, first surreptitiously visiting his home to overhear what his aunt has to say about him, then arranging a grand entry in the middle of the boys' funeral service. These two further incidents are essentially repetitions of that original mirror-experience, a reworking of the theme of self-discovery through a vision of oneself as seen by others, further stages in the development of the ego.

Part of the process of self-discovery at the time of the mirror-stage is the realization of sexual differentiation. The phallus is for Lacan not only the signification of this differentiation but also the signifier of all signification, the origin of all displaced social meaning. It is not altogether surprising, then, to find that the boys pitch their camp under a great sycamore, the towering representative of their newfound freedom.

But in Lucan, the mirror-stage is not without its accompaniment of guilt. At about the same time that the child learns to recognize himself as a separate being he is also learning that the intervention of the father compels him to distance himself from his mother, to separate himself, for ever, from that primal abundance. Shamefaced desire seeking elsewhere for its satisfaction is henceforward to be his lot, and he is to be driven from his Eden by the threat of his father's wrath.

When the boys first hear the firing of the shot they imagine it may be thunder; Huck speaks in an 'awed voice' (p. 97). Feeling guilty about the purloined food they brought with them to the island, they say their prayers 'lest they might call down a sudden and special thunderbolt from Heaven' (p. 92). Finally, thunder does arrive in reality, their tent is blown away, and various trees, including the one under which they had been sheltering, are riven by lightening. Once the father's anger has been visited on them in this way they recognize that the time has come to end their stay on the island, to leave the perpetually available gratifications of maternal sustenance, and return to the society which waits to claim them.

Once they arrive home, psychological significance again takes precedence over any naturalistic considerations of plausibility. Though Tom is cuffed as well as cuddled that evening, the community welcomes them back; even Huck is accorded the kind of greeting he would never normally expect from anyone. The succeeding chapters then show Tom in a series of participations in the activities of the small town, each of which is in some way provisional and unsatisfactory. Again it may be profitable to turn to Lacan to consider why this may be so.

Lacan terms the stage which follows the mirror-stage the experience of the symbolic order. Language itself is of course the primary mediator of this, and Lacan's theories may be considered to take language as their subject matter just as much as they take the psyche. It is at this point, therefore, that it becomes profitable to turn once more to some of the theorists that we considered earlier, and, in particular, to Derrida and Macherey.

If Tom is now firmly in the grip of language, and of all the social structures and pressures which operate in and through language, then what he will naturally attempt to do will be to use language as a medium of signification. But this is easier said than done. Even in Saussurean terms, the web of contrasts and differences is something which precedes the speaker's existence, and will doubtless continue after it. At least, though, submission to this system (for that is what it amounts to, like a good many social contracts) provides access to the mechanisms of power, and enables the speaker to perform the business of signification. The thrust of Derrida's criticism, though, was that signifier and signified are not in fact held in this fixed if extended relationship, that the business of producing meaning is like an inconvenient sum that always yields a remainder. If, as Lacan suggested, the unconscious is structured like a language, then the converse is also true.

Moreover, Tom is, so to say, spoken as well as speaking. His role is not something that he can independently determine, any more than he could

voluntarily decide what language he was going to speak. Just as, to use
Althusser's famous example, if a policeman in the street shouts 'Hey,
you!', we all turn round, each of us thinking that he or she is the person
who has just been named and identified, so Tom's identity as a subject in
his community is something into which he is called by the differing
ideologies whose interaction variously produces what he fondly might
consider to be his freely-arrived-at or independently-given subjective
consciousness.

What takes place in the story after Tom's return is, by the standards of
the little town, a series of major public events. The school puts on its
'Examination' day, a kind of public concert; a temperance movement,
which involves marching and the wearing of regalia, is formed; a revivalist
campaign takes the town by storm; Muff Potter is tried on the charge of
murdering the doctor. Education, temperance, religion, the law—a more
comprehensive list of Ideological State Apparatuses it would be hard to
find in the compass of a fairly short novel.

Tom's role in each of these is significant. The 'Examination' involves
the recitation of a good deal of purple poetry and even more colourful
prose. Tom, given a passage to recite from memory, approaches it with
great élan, but dries up in the middle and retires discomfited. He is
attracted by the uniforms worn by the Cadets of Temperance but, finding
that an opportunity to wear his at a funeral is denied him when the
sufferer inconsiderately recovers, he leaves the movement, only to find
that a sudden relapse means that the funeral takes place after all. His
principal reason for wanting to leave the organization had been that he
found its prohibition on swearing unendurable, though, freed from its
constraints once more, he finds that he is no longer under any great
impulsion to swear. An attack of measles prevents him from catching the
even more virulent strain of revivalism that is abroad, but on his return to
his friends he finds that he cannot participate in their pious citation of
scriptural texts. A thunderstorm that night (another thunderstorm!)
makes him think that he is individually singled out for the divine wrath
but, finding he has not been struck down after all, he postpones being
born again, and finds that his friends' enthusiasm has also waned.

In each of the cases I have listed here, Tom is unable to participate
successfully in the appropriate discourse. He dries up in the first, lacks
patience and the capacity to moderate his vocabulary in the second, and is
excluded by force of circumstances, and his own drives towards various
kinds of gratification, from the third. As a result he is finally in a state of
considerable alienation from his surroundings, though, like Althusser's
passer-by who is hailed by the policeman, he feels a sense of personal
identification in what is in reality a general social process. This is best
exemplified by his response to the thunderstorm:

> . . . he had not the shadow of a doubt that all this hubbub was about him. He
> believed that he had taxed the forbearance of the powers above to the

extremity of endurance, and that this was the result. It might have seemed to him a waste of pomp and ammunition to kill a bug with a battery of artillery, but there seemed nothing incongruous about the getting up of such an expensive thunderstorm as this to knock the turf from under an insect like himself.   (p. 134)

I cheated slightly in describing the law as an Ideological State Apparatus, since this would apply only to the civil law, and Muff Potter's is of course a criminal case. Nevertheless, this is finally the occasion on which Tom finds his voice—or, rather, the voice which the dominant ideology of his society wishes to hear him speak. In the period before the trial 'Every reference to the murder sent a shudder to his heart, for his troubled conscience and his fear almost persuaded him at these remarks were put forth as "feelers"' (p. 134). Finally, despite his fear of being murdered by Injun Joe, he contacts the defence counsel and offers himself as a witness. When called in court, he finds at first that 'the words refused to come' (p. 140) but gradually 'his words flowed more and more easily' (p. 141), as, providing the evidence that the court now wishes to hear, he fully finds his voice within his society for the first time.

In drawing attention to these features of the text, I am, it may be suggested, acting like the sculptor finding Abraham Lincoln in the middle of the lump of stone, or like a participant in one of Fish's seminars, reading into an effectively blank text whatever the interpretive community to which I may belong would expect me to find there. If this is so, then my denials of the suggestion would of course have no validity whatsoever, since they would emanate from within the very structure whose effectiveness I was attempting to deny. What is there left to appeal to for a definitive pronouncement on the issue? As far as Mark Twain is concerned, we cannot 'send for the man and ask him', since not only is this particular author dead, but The Author is dead also, deprived of any unique control over the meaning(s) of his work. It may be then that the meanings I am offering you are part and parcel of one particular ideology of literature that sits more or less easily with other ideologies and is effectively irreconcilable with others—all a part of a kind of intellectual game of poker, the greatest game in town, that turns up in someone's house all the time when least expected.

I think I incline to a slightly less radical explanation than this. A word can in theory be used to signify anything, but in practice is only used to signify a certain number of things, and the same may hold for this novel as well. Mark Twain was writing under the pressure of considerable emotional forces when providing a fictionalized version of his own childhood environment and experiences, and it seems reasonable to suppose that something akin to the psychological pressures that forced him to re-live his own early years would also shape his depiction of the way he represented them. If the Lacanian account of ego development has any validity, then, it will not be altogether surprising if it also provides a

framework for the representation of the same processes when an imagin-
ative writer is working under some emotional pressure. After all, very
similar features can be found in, for instance, the childhood sections of
novels by Dickens that bear in some way upon his own early experiences.

Twain, despite his nostalgia, was himself deeply alienated from many
of the adult discourses that he met in his youth. This is represented most
directly when he asserts that the turgid prose and poetry ascribed to the
'artistic' young ladies on 'Examination' day are in fact taken from a real
book published by an authentic example of the species. It is also known
that his dislike of religion was covertly a good deal stronger than the
relatively harmless quips he permitted himself in print would suggest.
Thus equipped, he would have little difficulty in providing an account of
these discourses that enables me to make the comments I have just
offered.

But, of course, the analysis I have been trying to offer cannot in the end
be simply collapsed back into an espousal of authorial intention. I have
argued that there are contradictions and silences within the book, just as
the society in which Twain was located was a divided and developing one.
Taking up these two points from Macherey, I have also suggested that
there are contradictions between the novel and society—both the society
in which it was composed, and the society in which it has the potential to
be read. Some of these, I have suggested, can form the basis for work with
relatively young pupils, and there would certainly be little logic in discon-
tinuing it with older ones.

The one feature of Twain's narrative that I have not so far explicitly
addressed in this chapter is that of the second symbolic death, namely
Tom's and Becky's misadventure in the cave. I suggested that the paradox
of the first one was that it actually constituted Tom's rite of passage into
the community of the living, that it provided him with a role into which
adult society was calling him. This second death is in many ways rather
more like the real thing. The predominant imagery throughout is that of
time; the children's scurryings to escape before the candles give out, their
attempt to make their food and energy last as long as possible. Set against
this is the timespan of millenia, which the curiously discordant passage (as
it superficially appears) spells out for us.

Time, in so far as it is measured out in homely days and hours, is an
entity that is called into existence by our process of signification. Time, in
so far as it is something that brings about our deaths and those of galaxies,
is something that may be said to signify us, infinitely beyond the reach of
our imagining and defining. In the progress of the narrative through the
cave these two processes are brought into juxtaposition, and the first is
annihilated.

In terms of narrative flow, we are then returned to Tom's escape, the
death of Injun Joe, the acquisition of the treasure, and a generally upbeat
ending; Tom's place within society is now assured. There is however a
parodic version of this in Huck's virtual rejection of the process, despite

his superficial acquiescence; he refuses to be interested in the acquisition of anything that is not required for the immediate satisfaction of bodily needs. His adoption by Widow Douglas never looks like being anything more than a temporary arrangement, despite Tom's attempts to resurrect the discourse of romantic robbery. Twain's statements in his 'Conclusion' are in effect a recognition that the ground has been cut from beneath any possible resolution:

> So endeth this chronicle. It being strictly the history of a boy, it must stop here; the story could not go on much further without becoming the history of a man.   (p. 198)

I have tried to suggest that it is possible for certain applications of literary theory to 'go on' much further than this, to lay bare what the text does not say and cannot say, as well as what it does and, as part of the same process, to make certain aspects of the context in which the reading takes place visible as well.

8 Ends and means

There are, as I am well aware, a number of ironies in the line of argument I have been following through this book. I have been pressing the case for a radical, relevant, analytical, action-oriented practice to be entitled the study of English, and the prime example of a text that I have chosen is historical rather than contemporary, nostalgic rather than forward-looking, foreign rather than domestic. In part, as I indicated earlier, this was in order to select an example that would be familiar to as many readers as possible, but there is more to it than that. To begin with, just as there is no reason why the Devil should have all the best tunes, so there is no reason why conservative empiricists should have all the best stories. *Tom Sawyer*, it may be worth reminding ourselves, is one of those books that young readers in significant numbers actually enjoy reading, and to promote that pleasure, and to latch on to it in order to produce further outcomes, are both desirable goals.

But pleasure is not a constant in the situation. Turning a book from an object for private gratification into something that is collectively studied in a school context is a not insignificant modification in itself. But the book that is read by a British pupil is not the same as the one that is read by an American one and, in the same way, the meanings that are generated by it in the twentieth century are not the same as those it provoked in the nineteenth. There are both advantages and disadvantages to this effective distancing of the reader from the work. If there are effectively no reference points for the reader at all in the text she will rapidly become bored and disaffected. *Tom Sawyer*, in its account of the childhood experiences of home, school, and society, is sufficiently familiar in its subject matter to avoid that danger at least. However, the retreat to an idyllic and superabundant natural existence on an island, stripped by the discourse of the novel of all previous inhabitants and all markers of current human activity and development, is not something that can be offered by contemporary

British writing—it could not happen in *Kes*, for example. Indeed, there is a whole history of British books that were either written for children or co-opted for this purpose, from *Robinson Crusoe* to *Coral Island* to *Treasure Island* to *Swallows and Amazons* to *Lord of the Flies*, that specifically show that an apparently untouched island nature is in fact written through with the signs of previous human habitation. In fact, where Golding, as indiated in a subsequently-written introduction to his novel, thought he was departing from this tradition, we can assert that he was most in conformity with it.

Tom Sawyer, then, presents the British reader in the 1980s with a seeming option that is no longer available; this is a part of its attraction as a classroom text. By its very distance from the life of its readers it creates a grid of interpretation that draws out meanings from both the book that is being studied and the lives of those that are studying it. This was the kind of experience that Iser was referring to when writing of gaps or indeterminacies in the text which raise the reader's presuppositions into consciousness.

The point that I am making here helps to illustrate, I believe, the way in which the analysis of literature is an activity that is different in kind from the type of direct involvement in human activity that was envisaged both by the advocates of 'Dialectical Materialism' (socialist realists such as Lukács) and the more directly interventionist strategies of a writer/critic like Brecht. The latter wrote a series of responses to Lukács in 1938 that he obviously found it prudent not to publish. In them he disclaimed the techniques of nineteenth-century novelists such as Tolstoy or Balzac, which he dismissively described as 'massing all manner of personal conflicts in long, expensive drawing-room scenes' (p. 70) in order both to concentrate on more expressionist techniques of writing and to illustrate the fact that the social context in which twentieth-century figures operate is larger than the family and the drawing-room. As a strategy whereby a writer in the 1930s should make his work perceptibly relevant to his audiences, this is hard to fault. Most of these, like most of the pupils we are considering, lacked any experience of drawing-rooms and whatever may go on in them. Moreover, the social determinants of individual characteristics are indeed, as Brecht suggests, rather different:

> For example in contemporary New York, not to mention Moscow, woman is less 'formed' by man than in Balzac's Paris; she is less dependent on him. So far this is quite simple. Certain struggles 'to a fever-pitch' therefore cease; other struggles which take their place (naturally others do take their place) are just as fierce but perhaps less individualistic. Not that they have no individual characteristics, for they are fought out by individuals. But allies play an immense part in them, such as they could not in Balzac's time.
>   (p. 79)

To examine the features to which Brecht refers, it is certainly desirable that fiction chosen for use in schools should illustrate the 'formation' of women in a contemporary context, and should depict in some way the significance that allies have in this process of formation. But there is also a place within the literature curriculum for the kind of text that shows a woman confined to house and home, her personality totally formed by these very precise social expectations, and denied by the processes of the narrative the opportunity to run away to an island, to lead her boy-friend to escape from a cave, or to show any solidarity with her classmates in the way that Tom does. Teaching, unlike drama in the way in which it intervenes in social processes, can suspend judgement in order to re-introduce it more effectively.

I am therefore arguing for a place on the literature syllabus for books that are not 'relevant' as the term is frequently used and understood; I am however equally insistent that relevance, in the ways in which I have outlined it, should be an outcome of the teaching process. Implicit in all that I have written is a rejection of the notion that there exists a canon of great works of literature whose effect on the reader, within a properly conducted educational establishment at least, is automatically morally beneficial. Instead, I am suggesting that the pedagogy of such institutions is an extremely powerful force which can well itself yield interesting material for study. The classification and framing of knowledge within an English lesson, when there is so little than can count as 'knowledge' in a quasi-positivist way, is a fascinating area in its own right, and it is perhaps naïve to imagine that pupils taught in such a context have not, in some more or less intuitive way, always carried out that kind of exercise anyway. After all, all analyses of teaching strategies are written by people who were themselves at some point pupils.

But, though I am rejecting the idea that a combination of text and teaching establishment automatically produces particular outcomes, I am certainly not suggesting that there are no outcomes to be found. You do not, so to speak, have to have been a subscriber to 'The Use of English' to believe that English has its uses. There was always one curious unin-tended outcome of what Eagleton has termed the 'left-Leavisite' position with regard to textual study. In theory it taught the Great Tradition to transmit certain core values, and it taught the study of advertisements in order to illustrate the corrupting effects of language used for base capital-ist motives, which thereby corrupted the pure springs of human discrimi-nation. In practice, though, such a method of teaching generated a powerful subjective impression in anyone graduating from it that he was now equipped to analyse *any* piece of text, no matter what its source was. This was, then, a kind of structuralist narratology *avant la lettre*, handi-capped only by the absence of any real method capable of being described to a sceptic: 'Either you see it or you don't', was a response that was often uttered with more force than effect. To be able to offer pupils this sense of power over their environment seems a desirable goal, especially if the sense of power is more than a delusion and can lead in some way to an effect on the pupil's environment.

What I am in effect saying is that literary theory is about more than just literature, which in any case is an entity that it is impossible to define. Again the reader may perhaps feel that we have all trodden this way before; after all, the lyrics of Bob Dylan were studied in class by pupils whose hair is now grey. However, I am not convinced that they were studied as aspects of a signifying process, and the use of theory, I have been suggesting, is crucial to the use of literature. To feel that you are able to say something about the workings and effects of a nineteenth-century novel, a pop lyric, a Jacobean play, a Clint Eastwood film, a Great War poem and a soap opera is a good experience; to be able to demonstrate this feeling in terms of actual practice is even better.

One move in this direction would consist of a general reassessment of those parts of the curriculum that are now beginning to be described, on school timetables as well as in volumes of theory, as aesthetics. The drive towards a co-ordinated programme of work in this area is altogether admirable but, if its effect is simply to demarcate a field in which personal expression is uniquely but temporarily privileged, then we will have seen no more than a wall of greater circumference going up around the same old ghetto. What I have in mind is something more like the old project that arose out of Saussure's original conceptions and was followed through in the early phase of structuralism: a study of the business of signification in all its aspects, with, in the original model at least, linguistics installed in the centre as the type of all communicative systems.

Linguistics cannot now be held to have this centrality since the assault of post-structuralists such as Derrida broke the bond between signifier and signified, but the study of discursive practices seems at least as capable of occupying the kind of key role I have described. It is for this reason that I would not wish to see aesthetics, in its new and broader definition, confined to dealing with nothing more than expressions of subjectivity, since this would unnecessarily separate it from the possible forms of analysis of these activities. 'English', as a curricular entity in the school curriculum, is capable of fulfilling a pivotal role between a widened aesthetics and a re-theorized social studies.

After all, the kinds of analysis we have been looking at are by no means confined in their application to the study of fiction. If Barthes was right in asserting the universality of narrative, then a news bulletin can be looked at as much as a novel, and a polemic as much as a poem. The current definition of literature, after all, is much narrower than was the case 300 years ago, and there is no effective reason why it should not be stretched once more or, rather, abandoned altogether if need be.

One way of effecting a change in the definition of literature within the classroom is to reassess what its position should be within a curriculum subject which is labelled 'English' and glossed as 'the English language' or 'language'. If such a subject takes as its given field of study the whole gamut of signifying practices, then 'literature', in a re-defined form, can more satisfactorily be located within it. Language, in the way I am using the term here, amounts to much more than a study of linguistic utterances taken in isolation. The point can best be made through comments on the nature of language activity in general written, probably by Bakhtin, under the name of Volosinov more than fifty years ago:

> *Any utterance*, no matter how weighty and complete in and of itself, *is only a moment in the continuous process of verbal communication*. But that continuous, verbal communication is, in turn, itself only a moment in the continuous, all-inclusive generative process of a given social collective. An important problem arises in this regard: the study of the connection between concrete verbal interaction, and the extraverbal situation–both the immediate situation, and, through it, the broader situation. The forms this connection takes are different, and different factors in a situation may, in association with this or that form, take on different meanings (for instance, these connections differ with the different factors of situation in literary or in scientific communications). Verbal communication can never *be understood and explained outside of this connection with a concrete situation*...In its concrete connection with a situation, verbal communication is always accompanied by social acts of a non-verbal character (the performance of labour, the symbolic acts of a ritual, a ceremony etc.), and is often only an accessory to these acts, merely carrying out an auxiliary role. *Language acquires life and historically evolves precisely here, in concrete verbal communication, and not in the abstract linguistic system of language forms, nor in the individual psyche of speakers.*   (1929, p. 95 emphasis as original)

There is not, then, a literary language and a scientific language (to take Volosinov's two examples) except in the relatively trivial sense that certain lexical items will turn up more frequently in one passage than in another. Part of the project undertaken by 'English' should therefore be to attend to 'concrete verbal interaction' in its various manifestations, recognizing in so doing that language may well not be the most important activity undertaken in any given 'concrete situation'. In a way, this may be described as a version of 'language across the curriculum', but I hope it will be recognized that what I am discussing works from rather stronger theoretical positions than some work that has been undertaken under that heading in recent years.

Of course, as this book has taken some care to point out, the 'concrete verbal interaction' that consists of reading a piece of literature varies across time, and from person to person, and Volosinov's comments should therefore be taken as applying to each specific instance rather than as erecting a specious generalization that might be held to apply to all readings of a particular volume. This indeed is the strength of his position. The 'abstract linguistic system of language forms' could well have been his phrase for structuralist approaches to literature, and 'the individual psyche of speakers' for the focus of those forms of reader-response theory that treat the reader as a social isolate; the comments he offers us are relevant enough, despite the fact that he preceded these two movements by so many years.

Other comments made by Volosinov also relate to the fact that a reader, over a period of time, reads not one book but several. There is therefore an interaction between these different readings, as well as between the various things read and the person who reads them. If each reading is regarded as a context, then how are they regarded, asks Volosinov, by people working in the 'abstract objectivist' tradition of Saussure?

> These contexts are thought of as forming a series of circumscribed, self-contained utterances all pointed in the same direction. In actual fact, this is far from true: contexts of usage for one and the same word often contrast with one another. The classical instance of such contrasting contexts of usage for one and the same word is found in dialogue. In the alternating lines of a dialogue, the same word may figure in two mutually clashing contexts. Of course, dialogue is only the most graphic and obvious instance of varidirectional contexts. Actually, any real utterance, in one way or another, makes a statement of agreement with or a negation of something. Contexts do not stand side by side in a row, as if unaware of one another, but are in a state of constant tension, or incessant interaction and conflict.
>
> (p. 80)

This dialogic interaction, then, is twofold: between book and book, and between text and reader. In a classroom context, there is a further possibility, and that is the way in which a dialogue can ensue between what a pupil reads and what she writes. From all that I have been arguing up till now, it should be clear that it will be difficult to think of this as pure spontaneous utterance, proceeding from the individual psyche of the writer. Instead it will be a prime example of intertextuality, shot through with all the features of the home and school contexts in which it is prepared, and also with all the traces of the previous reading that has been carried out. These are not excrescences, unfortunate features to be excused or glossed over, but are instead very much what the practice of writing in schools should be about. To this extent, then, the writing of pupils can be treated as parodic, like any other example of literature, adopting the appearances of ordinary discourse whilst lacking the referent that would be the expected feature of other instances of language production. But, though it is this, it is also more than this: as, so to speak, a line of dialogue in the conversation with other texts, it is also an intervention, a commentary, and an opening of a space.

My final illustrative example in this book is an utterly trivial one. In 1916 Frieda and D. H. Lawrence were living in Cornwall under less than ideal conditions in a series of rented cottages. She was the child of a German aristocratic family, he had bad health, which prevented him from fighting in a war they both hated and were glad to escape from as much as possible. Their correspondence with friends included letters to and from Lady Ottoline Morrell, who was a very grand lady indeed. Lady Ottoline sent them a counterpane as a present, but the accompanying letter arrived before the gift itself. Poring over what was obviously poor handwriting, the Lawrences detected a reference to a 'countrypair'.

He was busy trying to see *The Rainbow* into print. They were both at this point driven by a strong urge towards monogamy, in contrast to the more promiscuous habits of most of their correspondents, and felt that they had just arrived at a point in their relationship where, in what might have seemed to others a boring fashion, they had no need of others. Their physical distance from the Oxford–London–Cambridge triangle intensified this feeling of physical and mental remoteness. All things considered, then, it is small wonder that they should have read the word as 'countrypair', though it is unclear from his letter of reply how many of these implications Lawrence actually picked up.

It is however a perfect instance of an over-determined misreading, a recognition of themselves in what someone else might have written but did not. The term itself also seems, to me if not to them, like a demented piece of intertextuality, as though the polymorphous world of Joyce's *Ulysses* were breaking into the more unidirectional drive of *The Rainbow*.

With the resources of literary theory at his command, Lawrence might have been able to spell out some of these conclusions. He would have learnt something about the text, and more about himself. A teacher might have been able to do something about Lady Ottoline's handwriting, but I suspect the latter was far too much of an aristocrat to have bothered about it. And all the while Lawrence was writing what his letter of reply, referring to *The Rainbow*, called noiseless bullets to explode in people's souls.

Recommended further reading

The following brief list of recommendations consists mainly of secondary sources that may be readily obtained and that are introductory rather than specialist in character. It is intended as supplementary to the mainly primary sources cited in the text, and includes certain topics, the principal one being feminist theory, that appear implicitly rather than explicitly in this book. Most of the books listed here themselves contain helpful and detailed suggestions for further reading within the area that they cover.

General

EAGLETON, T. (1983) *Literary Theory*, Oxford, Blackwell.
   A witty, accessible, and stimulating survey of the field.
JEFFERSON, A. and ROBEY, D. (eds) (1982) *Modern Literary Theory*, London, Batsford.
   A good general introduction, which includes chapters on Russian formalism and New Criticism.
SHARRATT, B. (1982) *Reading Relations*, Brighton, Harvester.
   Innovative in form as well as in content, this illuminates a large number of themes.

Narratology and structuralism

CULLER, J. (1975) *Structuralist Poetics*, London, Routledge and Kegan Paul.
   An early introduction to the field for English-speaking readers.
CULLER, J. (1976) *Saussure*, Glasgow, Collins.
   A helpful introduction to basic concepts.
CULLER, J. (1983) *Barthes*, Glasgow, Collins.
   A brief and rather schematic introduction.
HAWKES, T. (1977) *Structuralism and Semiotics*, London, Methuen.
   A useful general introduction which introduced much new material to English-speaking readers.

JAMESON, F. (1972) *The Prison-House of Language*, Princeton, Princeton University Press.
  A critical introduction to the connections between Russian formalism and structuralism.
KRISTEVA, J. (1981) *Desire in Language*, Oxford, Blackwell.
  A useful and representative selection of essays.
LAVERS, A. (1982) *Roland Barthes*, London, Methuen.
  A particularly helpful treatment of some of the later work.
POSNER, R. (1982) *Rational Discourse and Poetic Communication*, Berlin, Mouton.
  Starting from a position within semiotics, this proceeds to extend the bounds of the study of discourse.
RIMMON-KENAN, S. (1983) *Narrative Fiction*, London, Methuen.
  Particularly useful on Genette.
SONTAG, S. (ed.) (1982) *A Barthes Reader*, London, Jonathan Cape.
  A good introductory selection.
TODOROV, T. (ed.) (1982) *French Literary Theory Today*, Cambridge, Cambridge University Press.
  A representative collection of structuralist essays from the late 1960s and 1970s.

Reception and reader-response theory

ECO, U. (1979) *The Rôle of the Reader*, Bloomington, Indiana University Press.
  Relates readerly activity to a distinction between 'open' and 'closed' texts.
GADAMER, H. G. (1975) *Truth and Method*, London, Sheed and Ward.
  A historical survey of, and an original contribution to, the study of hermeneutics.
HOLUB, R. C. (1984) *Reception Theory*, London, Methuen.
  Good account both of precursors and of current debates.
INGARDEN, R. (1973) *The Cognition of the Literary Work of Art*, Evanston, Illinois, Northwestern University Press.
  Adopts a somewhat different position from those described in this section on the way in which a reader constitutes a work of art.
RUTHROF, H. (1981) *The Reader's Construction of Narrative*, London, Routledge and Kegan Paul.
  Somewhat influenced by Iser, and more so by Ingarden; argues that text is composed of interaction between presented world and presentational process.
SULEIMAN, S. and CROSMAN, I. (eds) (1980) *The Reader in the Text*, Princeton, Princeton University Press.
  A good anthology covering various positions.

Post-structuralism

CULLER, J. (1983) *On Deconstruction*, London, Routledge and Kegan Paul.
  Traces the development of certain strands of thought from France to America.

HARARI, J. V. (ed.) (1979) *Textual Strategies*, London, Methuen.
A representative selection of essays by French and American contributors.
LEITCH, V. B. (1983) *Deconstructive Criticism*, London, Hutchinson.
A wide-ranging account, thematically organized.
NORRIS, C. (1982) *Deconstruction*, London, Methuen.
Gives an account of origins in the work of Nietzsche; helpful introduction to work of American deconstructionists.
RABINOW, P. (ed.) (1984) *The Foucault Reader*, Harmondsworth, Penguin.
A representative anthology, including two interviews.
STURROCK, J. (ed.) (1979) *Structuralism and Since*, Oxford, Oxford University Press.
Brief introductions to the works of, amongst others, Derrida, Lacan, and Foucault.

The practice of teaching

BELSEY, C. (1980) *Critical Practice*, London, Methuen.
A general introduction to literary theory that also looks at some of its practical implications.
CENTRE FOR CONTEMPORARY CULTURAL STUDIES, University of Birmingham (1981) *Unpopular Education*, London, Hutchinson.
A survey of change and development in postwar education, with an analysis of some of the determinants involved.
HALL, S. *et al.* (eds) (1980) *Culture, Media, Language*, London, Hutchinson.
Relates practical teaching issues to theoretical questions concerning language and media studies.
WIDDOWSON, P. (ed.) (1982) *Re-reading English*, London, Methuen.
Looks at current practices and institutions influential as role models.

Feminist theory

BATSLEER, J. *et al.* (eds) (1985) *Rewriting English*, London, Methuen.
Examines the way gender is inscribed within texts.
FETTERLEY, J. (1979) *The Resisting Reader*, Bloomington, Indiana University Press.
Describes how a male role is prescribed for the reader by classic American fiction.
MARKS, E. and COURTIVRON, I. DE (eds) (1980) *New French Feminisms*, Brighton, Harvester.
A good selection of translated passages.
MOI, T. (1985) *Sexual/Textual Politics*, London, Methuen.
Contrasts Anglo-American and European traditions; good section on Kristeva.
RUTHVEN, K. K. (1984) *Feminist Literary Studies*, Cambridge, Cambridge University Press.
A wide-ranging and up-to-date survey.

References

References in the text cite the date of original publication. References listed hereunder follow the same convention, but then supply details, where possible, of an accessible version of each work in the English language. Page references are to this latter version throughout.

ALTHUSSER, L. (1970, trans. 1971) *Lenin and Philosophy and other essays*, New York, Monthly Review Press.

BAKHTIN. See VOLOSINOV.

BARTHES, R. (1957, trans. 1972) *Mythologies*, London, Jonathan Cape.

BARTHES, R. (1966, trans. 1977) *Introduction to the Structural Analysis of Narratives* in *Image–Music–Text*, Glasgow, Collins.

BARTHES, R. (1970, trans. 1974) *S/Z*, New York, Hill and Wang.

BARTHES, R. (1973a, trans. 1981) *Theory of the Text* in Young, R. (ed.) *Untying the Text*, London, Routledge and Kegan Paul.

BARTHES, R. (1973b, trans. 1981) *Textual Analysis of Poe's 'Valdemar'* in YOUNG, R. (ed.) *Untying the Text*, London, Routledge and Kegan Paul.

BOARD OF EDUCATION (1921) *The Teaching of English in England*, London, HMSO (the Newbolt Report).

BOOTH, W. C. (1961) *The Rhetoric of Fiction*, Chicago, University of Chicago Press.

BRECHT, B. (1938, trans. 1977) *Against Georg Lukács* in BLOCH, E. *et al.*, *Aesthetics and Politics*, London, New Left Books.

BREMOND, C. (1966) 'La logique des possibles narratifs', *Communications*, Paris, 8, pp. 60–76.

DEPARTMENT OF EDUCATION AND SCIENCE (1975) *A Language for Life*, London, HMSO (the Bullock Report).

DERRIDA, J. (1967a, trans. 1974) *Of Grammatology*, Baltimore, Johns Hopkins University Press.

DERRIDA, J. (1967b, trans. 1978) *Writing and Difference*, London, Routledge and Kegan Paul.

FISH, S. (1980) *Is There a Text in This Class?*, Cambridge, Mass., Harvard University Press.

FORSTER, E. M. (1924) *A Passage to India*, London, Edward Arnold.

FOUCAULT, M. (1969, trans. 1972) *The Archaeology of Knowledge*, London, Tavistock.

FOUCAULT, M. (1977) 'The eye of power', Preface to BENTHAM, J. *Le Panoptique*, Paris, Belfond.

FOUCAULT, M. (1982) Afterword in DREYFUS, H. L. and RABINOW, P. *Michel Foucault: beyond structuralism and hermeneutics*, Brighton, Harvester.

FRYE, N. (1957) *Anatomy of Criticism*, Princeton, Princeton University Press.

GENETTE, G. (1972, trans. 1980) *Narrative Discourse*, Oxford, Blackwell.

GREIMAS, A. J. (1973) 'Les actants, les acteurs et les figures' in CHABROL, C. (ed.) *Sémiotique Narrative et Textuelle*, Paris, Larousse.

ISER, W. (1976, trans. 1978) *The Act of Reading*, London, Routledge and Kegan Paul.

JAKOBSON, R. (1960) 'Closing statement: linguistics and poetics' in SEBOEK, T. A. (ed.) *Style in Language*, Cambridge, Mass., MIT Press.

JAUSS, H. R. (1970, trans. 1982) *Toward an Aesthetic of Response*, Minneapolis, University of Minnesota Press.

JEROME, J. K. (1889, rep. 1957) *Three Men in a Boat*, Harmondsworth, Penguin.

KRISTEVA, J. (1970) *Le Texte du Roman*, The Hague, Mouton.

LACAN, J. (1966, trans. 1977) *Écrits*, London, Tavistock.

LEAVIS, F. R. (1969) *English Literature in Our Time and the University*, London, Chatto and Windus.

LÉVI-STRAUSS, C. (1955, trans. 1968) *Structural Anthropology*, Harmondsworth, Penguin.

LODGE, D. (1975) *Changing Places*, London, Secker and Warburg.

MACHEREY, P. (1966, trans. 1978) *A Theory of Literary Production*, London, Routledge and Kegan Paul.

MACHEREY, P. and BALIBAR, É. (1978) 'Literature as an ideological form; some Marxist propositions', *The Oxford Literary Review*, Oxford, 3, pp. 4–12. Rep. in PUGH, A. K. *et al.* (eds) (1980) *Language and Language Use*, London, Heinemann Educational.

MACHEREY, P. (1983) 'In a materialist way' in MONTEFIORE, A. (ed.) *Philosophy in France Today*, Cambridge, Cambridge University Press.

PRINCE, G. (1982) *Narratology*, Berlin, Mouton.

PROPP, V. (1928, trans. 1958) *Morphology of the Folktale*, Austin, University of Texas Press.

RIFFATERRE, M. (1966, trans. 1980) 'Describing poetic structures: two approaches to Baudelaire's *Les Chats*' in TOMPKINS, J. (ed.) *Reader-Response Criticism*, Baltimore, Johns Hopkins University Press.

TWAIN, M. (1876, rep. 1953) *The Adventures of Tom Sawyer*, London, Collins.

VOLOSINOV, V. N. (1929, trans. 1973) *Marxism and the Philosophy of Language*, London, Seminar Press.

Glossary

It should be noted that the definitions offered here relate only to the meanings of the terms as used in this book, and are not comprehensive dictionary entries.

Addressee
In Jakobson, the recipient of the speech event.
Addresser
In Jakobson, the utterer of the speech event.
Agonism
In Foucault, the struggle that ensues when power meets resistance.
Anachrony
In Genette, a narrative sequence relating to events outside the timespan of the narrative in question.
Analepsis
In Genette, a 'flashback' or account of an event prior to the narrative in question.
Autochthony
State of being earth-born rather than produced by parents; hence, aboriginal inhabitants of a locale.
Base
In Marxism, set of primary economic relations.
Catalyzer
In Barthes, narrative unit which is secondary to nuclei and fills in space between the latter.
Code
In Jakobson, set of symbols drawn on to produce a speech event.
Conative
In Jakobson, that aspect of a speech event which controls or influences the addressee.
Contact
In Jakobson, the physical medium involved in the transmission of a speech event.

Context
In Jakobson, the perception, held in common by addresser and addressee, of the relevant features of the setting of the speech event.

Cultural
In Barthes, the code that represents the shared knowledge of the workings and beliefs of a society.

Diachronic
Relating to change or development through time, as opposed to synchronic.

Dialectical
In Marxism, relating to the conflict of forces that precipitates historical change.

Ellipsis
In Genette, the omission of a period of time during a narrative.

Emotive
In Jakobson, that aspect of a speech event which describes the mental state of the addresser.

Formalism
The study of the devices by which literature is marked out as distinct from more directly functional language uses.

Hermeneutic
In Barthes, the code that deals with the creation and resolution of puzzles or mysteries.

Heterodiegetic
In Genette, a narrative sequence relating to a different theme from that of the narrative in question.

Homodiegetic
In Genette, a narrative sequence relating to the same theme as the narrative in question.

Horizon of expectations
A shared system of beliefs and norms which a work of literature may either conform to or violate.

Ideation
In Iser, the mental creation of non-visual representations.

Indice
In Barthes, a unit of narrative which powerfully and necessarily generates information relating to characters or agents.

Informant
In Barthes, a narrative unit, weaker than an indice, which supplies information relating to the actors or the setting in a narrative.

Intercalated
In Genette, narrative technique whereby different sequences are intercut.

Iterative
In Genette, the telling once in a narrative of an event that is supposed to have occurred on two or more occasions.

Langue
In Saussure, the shared language system which is drawn on to create any individual 'parole'.

Lexia
In Barthes, a narrative unit which manifests the presence of one or more codes.

Logocentric
Attentive to words as being in some way a guarantee of authenticity.
Materialism
Belief that events in the world are generated by physical and hence social action, rather than by ideas.
Message
In Jakobson, information content of a speech event.
Metalingual
In Jakobson, that aspect of a speech event which deals with reflexively with the event itself.
Mirror stage
In Lacan, that period in a child's development when he acquires from others an image of himself as an integrated whole that he then attempts to adopt.
Narratology
The systematic study of the constituent elements of narrative structure.
Nucleus
In Barthes, a narrative unit that supplies a key unit of plot.
Oxymoron
An expression in which two terms are mutually contradictory.
Parole
In Saussure, an utterance as opposed to the whole system of language from which it is derived.
Phonocentric
Attentive to speech in preference to text as being in some way more authentic or less ambiguous.
Poetic
In Jakobson, that aspect of a speech event which is concerned with the way in which the message is delivered.
Proairetic
In Barthes, the code which relates to predicting the outcome of actions.
Prolepsis
In Genette, a 'flash-forward' or account of an event subsequent to the narrative in question.
Referential
In Jakobson, that aspect of a speech event which relates to the environment in which it occurs.
Semic
In Barthes, the code that provides information relating to people, places, objects etc.
Semiotics
The systematic study of symbolizing systems.
Signified
In Saussure, the concept denoted by the signifier.
Signifier
In Saussure, the spoken or written representation of a signified.
Singulative
In Genette, a type of narration which tells once what is alleged to have occurred once.

Superstructure
In Marxism, the system of beliefs and cultural practices in a society that is generated by the base.
Symbolic
In Barthes, the code that deals with structures of classification.
Synchronic
Those elements of a system that are contemporaneous at a given point in time.
Teleology
The belief in progress towards a predetermined end.

Index